Dancing in the Kitchen

Endorsements

"Falling in love is not unlike tripping as you step off a curb. It requires no effort. Staying in love through the challenges that life brings to every relationship is a different story. It does not come naturally. It is an art, a skill to be learned and practiced. What a thrill to fall in love. What a thrill to stay in love. Debbie Cunningham has captured the essence of that art and shares it in a creative and engaging way. No matter what your love relationship is right now, *Dancing in the Kitchen* is a book you can't afford to miss."

—Ken Davis,
Best-selling Author, Inspirational and Motivational Speaker,
www.kendavis.com

"Debbie beautifully captures stories from real couples who courageously faced the wilderness season of marriage while leaning into the pain of the dance together. *Dancing in the Kitchen* normalizes the trials that all couples will ultimately face by offering the hope that staying in love through the storm is possible."

—Melanie Eddy,
MSW, LCSW, Women's Counselor, Life Coach, Speaker, www.
encouragehercoachingandcounseling.com

"Dancing is a wonderful metaphor for the life of a couple in their marriage relationship. Two people moving together to the music intertwined in movement, grace, and passion. Often, I have used this as an illustration of marriage for a couple contemplating marriage. Debbie Cunningham does a wonderful job encouraging couples to see marriage as the high calling that it is. I have known Debbie, Derek, Deanna, and Drake for a number of years as one of their pastors in our church. I am happy to commend Debbie Cunningham to you and this book as a much-needed tool to encourage couples in their marriage."

—Pastor Mike Smith,
Christ Community Church

"Weddings make us weep with their fresh romance. A white-haired couple walking hand in hand makes us long for a marriage that stands the test of time. Debbie writes beautifully of the middle, where things can be hard, and a marriage can fail... or grow strong from the fight. This is a much-needed resource for a love-starved generation."

—Kim Woodward,
MSN, APRN, CPNP-PC-Pediatric Nurse Practitioner, Nashville, TN

"A valuable piece of work for anyone who wants to increase the opportunity for intimacy in their marriage and lay some groundwork for shifting the status quo. Debbie Cunningham encourages us to dance, create intimacy and love even when it's hard to find our rhythm; our moves serve to remind us we are clearly dance competition rejects and to keep on dancing even when we step on each other's toes. This is a great book with extremely helpful, actionable tips for people who want to make their love last."

—Janet Ivey,
Actress, Founder/Creator of Janet's Planet, Inc.

"Wow! *Dancing in the Kitchen* is such a great book... and an easy read in a conversational style. You will feel like you are having a cup of coffee with Debbie as she tells stories from her experiences and shares wisdom from God's Word. Read it and learn how to fight for your marriage!"

—Candy Davison,
Women's Ministry Coordinator Emeritus-Sandy Cove
Ministries

"Debbie Cunningham's book *Dancing in the Kitchen* is a must read for everyone who believes in love or who wants to believe in love. You will most likely find your story, as I did, in someone else's story. Debbie shows us how we can grow and learn through the good times and the rough times. She says it takes a lifetime to figure it all out. I totally agree but with Debbie's insight and wisdom, we can get renewed hope of how to dance in the kitchen."

—Sue Z. McGray,
Regional Director for Christian Women in Media Association,
Speaker,
Author of *Becoming Visible, Letting Go of the Things That
Hide Your True Beauty*

"It is obvious that marriage is under attack and even many good ones are in troubled waters. Debbie Cunningham is a woman of great passion and substance. She uses her music, and now her book, to bring truth and light to places that we can never know until heaven. *Dancing in the Kitchen* will inspire you to rehearse the steps and keep dancing in the arms of your love."

—Ellie Lofaro,
Author/International Speaker

"We encourage you to purchase and study this wonderful new book written by our dear friend Debbie Cunningham. Paula and I have been married for thirty-eight years, having gotten married at the ripe old age of twenty-one in 1980! We have known Debbie and her husband, Derek, for over thirty years now. We have seen them "live the life" that her book inspires us all to live. We can all learn to better enrich our marriages and relationships, no matter if we have been married for a day, a year, or decades. Debbie has a unique way of sharing the many lessons she has learned and lived in building her strong marriage with her best friend, Derek. They are an inspiration to us, and we look forward to more great books and more great music from Debbie!"

—Paul McCulloch,
Entrepreneur and
Paula McCulla,
Award winning singer /songwriter

"Debbie Cunningham has written a surprisingly delightful and insightful book. In a world where falling in love is often at the top of the to-do list, Debbie's book will help you stay in love— an achievement of nuance and courage—and, as *Dancing in the Kitchen* shows us, an achievement filled with surprise and unexpected joy! Make room for this book on your e-reader and your bookshelf. Make room for its words in your life. Give yourself a legacy of a love that lasts."

—Allison Allen,
Speaker and Author of *Shine: Stepping into the Role you Were Made For* / Credits include: Broadway, Women of Faith

"Debbie Cunningham's *Dancing in the Kitchen* is an exciting addition to the literature on marriage. It is the product of the author's deep dig into the trenches of the real day-to-day challenges couples face. Her analogy of learning the intricacies of the steps and moves of dancing is right on! She refers to mastering the steps of one dance and then the music changes. How true! It is filled with wisdom and nuggets that can be implemented immediately. As a marriage therapist for more than three decades and living in my own marriage for five decades, I highly recommend this book. *Dancing in the Kitchen* will teach and inspire you. It will be a place you will return again and again for help and hope."

—Margaret Phillips,
M.S. Licensed Marriage and Family Therapist, Author of *The*
Marriage Ark

Dancing in the Kitchen

Hope and Help for
STAYING IN LOVE

Debbie Cunningham

NASHVILLE

NEW YORK • LONDON • MELBOURNE • VANCOUVER

Dancing in the Kitchen

Hope and Help for Staying in Love

Published in New York, New York, by Morgan James Publishing. Morgan James is a trademark of Morgan James, LLC. www.MorganJamesPublishing.com

The Morgan James Speakers Group can bring authors to your live event. For more information or to book an event visit The Morgan James Speakers Group at www.TheMorganJamesSpeakersGroup.com.

All Scripture quotations, unless otherwise indicated, are taken from The Holy Bible, New International Version®, NIV®.

ISBN 9781642791211 paperback
ISBN 9781642791228 eBook
Library of Congress Control Number: 2018947258

Cover Design by:
Rachel Lopez
www.r2cdesign.com

Interior Design by:
Christopher Kirk
GFSstudio.com

In an effort to support local communities, raise awareness and funds, Morgan James Publishing donates a percentage of all book sales for the life of each book to Habitat for Humanity Peninsula and Greater Williamsburg.

Get involved today! Visit
www.MorganJamesBuilds.com

For all the couples out there struggling in the middle years of marriage.

May you rekindle the spark and learn to dance again.

Table of Contents

Foreword

If someone had told me when I got married fifty years ago that I would celebrate decades of anniversaries in my lifetime, I would probably have laughed. You see, most people would look at how I grew up and call it a "challenging" family situation, to say the least.

I never experienced having a father in the home. All the men in my extended family had been divorced out, so my life experience before marriage was completely female-dominated. I didn't see even one marriage that lasted. I had been "taught" (so to speak) that men were to be loathed, not trusted, and were only out to get one thing… and sadly, you can guess what that was. Truthfully, I had no idea what marriage was all about.

But I knew when I met Dan Miller on my first day at the Ohio State University campus, I had met someone I could trust. I liked him immediately. He became my best, and most trusted, friend. We married in 1968 and he remains my best, and most trusted, friend.

In fact, I have a little sign in my kitchen that states, "And They Lived Happily Ever After." It's a daily reminder to me that "happily ever after" is something we work towards… it's not just a fantasy.

I believe most every woman would like to be swept off her feet by her knight in shining armor and be treated like a princess for the rest of her life. It's what we learn as children reading fairytales. But I have yet to hear of even one princess who has led a problem-free, fairytale life—that only happens in movies and books.

In real life, marriage can be very difficult, and life can hit you in the face with great force.

Yes, Dan and I have experienced an amazing marriage but that doesn't mean it is trouble-free and every day is happy and harmonious. We have had some serious mountains to climb and some very low valleys to navigate. You can't live in the same house day in and day out with someone and not have anger, frustration, disappointment, and myriad other emotions come into play. It's how you handle those situations that makes the difference in maintaining a good relationship.

So, what makes a marriage thrive... and not just endure? I think Debbie hits the nail on the head when she compares marriage to dancing!

You think you learn all the right steps, then the music changes and you have to learn new steps, and then it all changes again. All along the way you're stepping on one another's toes, pulling apart when you should be embracing, and getting out of sync when you lose the beat. Learning to dance requires a lot of practice and a lot of patience. Just like marriage. The trouble is, many people simply don't care to work that hard. It seems easier to dump that partner and find a new, willing, and seemingly more experienced dancer.

Fortunately, Debbie points out that we can learn to "dance with the one who brung you"—as the old saying goes—and even have some spontaneous moments that take us by surprise and reassure us all is not lost.

Debbie lays out real-life examples where relationships have serious challenges, have seemingly failed miserably, and sometimes even appear to be irreparable. However, she also shows that, although many couples could have ended their relationships, it is totally possible to pick up the pieces and carefully put them back into place, making the bond even stronger.

When I was young, I naively thought that by the time I reached a certain age, I would have it all together and I could coast "happily ever after." But now that I have more than a few years of marriage under my belt, I find I am *still* learning to live with my husband. Yes, he remains my best friend, my lover, my confidant, and the best thing that ever happened to me. However, some days I simply want to throttle him!

Commitment is a big, strong word that flows throughout the pages of this book. We live in a time when commitment is often thrown to the wind at the slightest change in one's happiness. If Dan and I hadn't been intentional, every single day, about the commitment we have to one another, we would have followed the path of all the other couples in my family before the first year of our marriage was up!

My experience: Being intentional in your every day is essential to a happy life together. Ensuring that every encounter with one another ends in a "win-win" for each of you, even if you have to compromise, makes for enduring love.

In the pages that follow, Debbie masterfully steers you through how to maintain a healthy interconnectedness that doesn't take away from your own needs and dreams but enhances them through the love of God and His plan for your home and marriage. You will quickly get drawn into the stories, the song lyrics, and the experiences she lays out in the pages ahead.

I pray your reading leads you to a better understanding of how to dance in the kitchen and live *happily* ever after!

—**Joanne Fairchild Miller,**
Author, *Creating a Haven of Peace*

Acknowledgements

First and foremost, I praise God for this journey and *all* He has done. In a million years, I would have never expected to write a book on marriage. Only God can do immeasurably more than we ever ask or imagine for ourselves. For this and my salvation, I am eternally grateful. It is HIS work; I just show up and ask Him to flow through me.

To my husband: Derek, I could never have the courage to follow my heart without you by my side. Thank you for all your support and encouragement in my music career and this author journey. Thank you for loving me unconditionally, for always being my cheerleader and seeing the best in me even when I cannot. Thank you for a life and a marriage filled with laughter, forgiveness, and grace. I'm so thankful God gave us to one another at such a young age. You are my soulmate and best friend, and I am so grateful to do life with you. I love you with all my heart!

To my kids: Drake, Deanna, son-in-law Joseph: Thank you for all your encouragement and support as I wrote this book. I pray you will always remember to forgive everyday just as Jesus forgives us. *That alone* will forever change your relationships! Keep our tradition… by dancing in your own kitchens with those you love. Dad and I love you so much!

To my parents: Thank you for the example you are to me in your marriage, how you both serve one another and other people, tirelessly, without complaint! Mom, thank you for being a woman of strength, even when you were a single parent. Truly modeling for your children a woman who goes through hardship but instead of wallowing in despair, picks up and moves forward for the sake of herself and her children. Dad, thanks for choosing to be our dad. You may be a "stepparent" but you became "Dad" by your actions. I am grateful for the legacy you both have woven into our family and, most especially, to be your daughter.

To my Bible study group: You ladies have prayed me through every step of this process! I am so grateful for each of you in my life. Thank you for all your encouragement.

To Ann and Paula: You two are my very best friends. You have walked with me and prayed for me more than twenty-five years and I do not know where I'd be without your listening ears! Thank you for encouraging me throughout this process. Your friendship is a treasure.

To Karen Anderson: Thank you! This book truly would not be what it is without you. You were my cheerleader when it was just an idea—long before you were even working as my publisher. You prayed for me, encouraged me when I felt overwhelmed or inept, and challenged me to keep following God on this journey. Your advisement, counsel, and mentorship have been invaluable to me. I am grateful you see things I cannot see, and I trust your insight implicitly. I count your friendship to me over these many years as a true blessing.

To Sissi Haner: Thank you for your expertise. I am grateful for your editing and technical skills, especially because they are talents I seriously lack!

To David Hancock and the Morgan James staff: Thank you for publishing this book. I am so grateful you thought it was valuable enough to add to your roster. I look forward to a long partnership with you.

Last but not least, **THANK YOU to *all the couples* who so graciously shared their stories with me.** I know it is not always easy to re-live hard moments. May God truly bless each one of you for the encouragement you are bringing to others through your vulnerability and testimony.

Introduction

*There is no more lovely, friendly, and charming
relationship, communion, or company than a
good marriage.*

—Martin Luther

A s a jazz recording artist and songwriter, I have been singing
about love and romance for over a decade. That means I
sing songs that you have come to know as jazz standards, songs
like "The Way You Look Tonight," "'S Wonderful," "Fly Me to
the Moon," "My Funny Valentine," or "The Girl from Ipanema."
Stylistically, I am similar to artists like Tony Bennett, Peggy Lee,
or more recently, Diana Krall or Michael Bublé.

Because of that, I have met and spoken with couples from
every age and stage of life who enjoy music as a way of enrich-
ing their lives together. I've known couples married two weeks
and those celebrating sixty years. I've watched as couples snuggle
closely as they listen to me perform and I've seen couples sitting
at a dinner show on their smartphones with no conversation, completely oblivious to their spouse or the ambiance in the room. I
have also noticed as divorce rates have skyrocketed in our society.

Marriages are in crisis.

When I began to consider the implications of how we, as couples, could do better at staying in love, those thoughts began to show up in my songwriting. I started writing songs that reflected where I was in my life as a married woman. Songs that reflected the lightheartedness I desired in my marriage like "Kiss and Make Up," a song about forgiving and not holding grudges or "What Lovers Do," which reminds me to be intentional about romance. I wanted to write an album of songs that reflected the journey of committed love instead of songs about falling out of it. So, I did that with my album, *A Million Kisses*.[1]

During that same time period, I noticed the posts I was writing on my news blog also started reflecting my marriage and family life. Fans, strangers, and friends began to comment that I should write a book about marriage; I thought they were crazy! Although I have had a daily habit of journal writing for years, I never anticipated writing a book on marriage. Yet, it resonated deeply within my heart. I am passionate about encouraging couples to stay together and invest in their relationship.

I have been married for over thirty years to my high school sweetheart, Derek. And I'll tell you a secret. I had a crush on him when I was in seventh grade! Of course, he had no idea I existed. He was just the cute guy who played the berry saxophone in the jazz band and I was smitten. It wasn't until high school that we actually met. I was Liesl in *The Sound of Music* and he was playing in the pit band for our high school musical. Yes, I was sixteen and he was seventeen, and I guess the rest is history. We certainly have had ups and downs in our relationship as we matured together. I know it can be a challenge from experience. I deeply love my husband, and we are truly happily married. Not perfect mind you, but our intention is "until death do us part" as we said in our vows.

Over the years, I have watched many give up on those vows for multitudes of reasons and it grieves my heart. I'm not pronouncing judgment here, just an observation. I know many individuals who have gotten divorced; they never wanted one and tried their best to save the marriage, but their spouse chose a different path. I also know the hardship divorce brings into the lives of the couple (even if they have been miserable) and the painful, ripple effects it has on an entire family. My intention is only to encourage all of us to a better journey of staying in love. I mean, does anyone get married with the intention of divorce?

Marriage... two people coming together, physically, emotionally, and spiritually in unity for a lifetime. It takes a lifetime, I think, to figure it all out. Or at least in some seasons of marriage it feels that way. I adore my husband. But some days he drives me crazy and some days I drive him crazy. We love each other deeply but there are moments we don't like each other very much. That's okay... some days I don't like *me* either. That's just a reality. But when you have made a lifelong commitment and mean to keep it... how *do* you go about keeping it? You know, "for better for worse, in sickness and in health..." because you're going to have it all, whether you expect to or not. I need to be reminded of what it takes to stay in love, especially at this stage of the game. Mid-life, emptying nest, and dealing with all this aging nonsense! I must learn to laugh at the days to come because for better or worse, they are coming.

I dearly love my husband and I want it to stay that way.

I want to rekindle those moments of lightheartedness that we had when we first fell in love to connect us when days are not so lighthearted. I'm talking about being present to what we have in the moment and not taking each other for granted. Remembering the spontaneity and thoughtfulness that comes in the early days of relationship and stoking the fires on that. I am expecting that you would like that too.

Marriage is hard. Anyone who says otherwise is fooling himself or hasn't been married long enough to figure that out yet. As I have been living in this world, I am astounded as marriages fall apart by the dozens. Friends, colleagues, and family alike, married more than twenty, even thirty, years closing the door on their relationships. Certainly, any relationship that lasts more than one day has the propensity to stretch you beyond your limits, but it can also be an AMAZING adventure that two people enjoy for a lifetime. In it you will scale mountains and descend into valleys deep. At times, you will experience uncertainty as you travel the great unknown of your spouse and discover things about each other that you hadn't expected. But there are also beautiful moments and mountaintop seasons of euphoria from emotional, spiritual, and physical intimacy that only comes when two people selflessly invest in each other.

And there will be deserts. BIG deserts... seasons dry of emotion, dry of giving, dry of selflessness because one or both of you are spent. You are empty and burnt out and just need rest, food, or refreshment for your own longing soul. You will wish for the mountain air and the joyful pastures when your relationship was easier. But you must climb the mountain to reach its peak, and it is not for the faint of heart. Yet, when you get to the mountaintop, it is WORTH everything it took to become one and to live in unity. It takes investment to truly get to the places of learning, to hike the terrain, hanging on with all you've got and spurring each other on to make it together. I believe it is worth it. Do you? Do you want to believe?

My most favorite prayer in Scripture is from Mark 9:24, "I believe, help me overcome my unbelief!"

At some level, I pray it daily about one thing or another. Its power lies in the reliance on God alone changing our perspective. I want to believe God, to trust Him and his Word instead of my human, often limited, vision of His power. I forget that anything is possible if God is doing the work. We can start there, asking for faith to believe and God will lead us through the rest, my friend. He will do the work in our marriages if we will allow Him to do it. I believe that staying in love long-term is possible even through the hard circumstances that come into our lives. I have found in my experience, and the experiences of the couples I interviewed, that this kind of love is worth the effort and worth celebrating. Will you join me in this journey? If you want that, then turn to the pages ahead and read the stories of others who have also struggled. But first, let us start together by praying...

We believe, Lord, but help us in our unbelief. As we seek your wisdom, thank you for what you will do to transform our marriage into a lifetime of staying in love. In Jesus' name, Amen.

A Million Kisses

Lyrics and music by Debbie Cunningham

I want a million kisses kind of love
The kind that every woman and little girl
Is dreaming of
That kind of romance doesn't come from one night
But through days and years, happiness and tears
Until things work out right
Hand in hand walking through the rain or with stars up above
I want a million kisses kind of love

The kind that dances in the kitchen
When the skies are turning gray
The one that holds you oh so tight
When the blues just won't go away

I want a million kisses kind of love
The kind that embraces the seasons
Real life is made of
That kind of romance still makes me swoon
From the first light of day, seeing your face
Till shadows are cast by the moon
Hand in hand, walking through the rain or with stars up above
I want a million kisses, I want a million kisses
I want a million kisses kind of love

CHAPTER ONE

Dancing in the Kitchen

*Life isn't about waiting for the storm to pass... It's about
learning to dance in the rain.*

—*Vivian Greene*[2]

I am convinced that most of us want the kind of love relationship that is described in my song, "A Million Kisses." I wrote
the song while I was pondering that thought. In fact, I wrote an
entire album of songs dedicated to that pondering. What does real
love look like over a lifetime —the highs, the lows, and the celebration of it all—in a committed relationship? What keeps us
moving forward, fighting for the love we once knew early on but
has grown flat in the hard seasons? We desire love that is joyful
and tender, that ignites passion but also lightheartedness, like a
dance when life is good yet still has strong arms to envelop us
when the world comes crashing down. It does not come from a
one-night stand, nor even from mutual attraction but from commitment and companionship. It grows, as we are present to one
another in individual moments of everyday living. It flourishes,
as we are intentional to cultivate our relationship even when skies
are gray. Maybe you are thinking you want that too but really

don't know how to get back to that again? There is no one path, but I think we can change the landscape of our marriages if we get serious about moving in that direction. This isn't an all or nothing exercise. This is a journey of trial and error. Consequently, you have to decide to start somewhere so that your course changes its current trajectory.

So, what do I mean by the phrase "dancing in the kitchen"? It's not actually about dancing, although it can be! It is about capturing spontaneity and connection with your spouse for a brief moment, counterintuitive to whatever is happening at the time. It is easy to have a connection when things are going well in your relationship, but how do we connect when life is stressful and chaotic? Or you have grown apart? When we first fall in love, we steal moments together: a peck on the cheek, a quick hug. We purpose to make the gray days less gray for each other. We cultivate these little unexpected moments of kindness and thoughtfulness even when things go wrong. What if we could learn to do that again? Intentionally recapturing the spontaneity of love? I know intentional and spontaneous seem to be opposites but stay with me.

Picture this scenario: you have had a long stressful day, the sink is filled with dishes, kids need help with homework, you still need to make dinner, and your husband walks through the door after his stressful day. Or you have had a long stressful day at your office and come home to chaos. You can verbally explode about the frustrations you have both encountered today or one of you can pull up your favorite song on your smartphone or turn on the radio, grab your spouse, and have a little dance. Just for a moment or two. You can say something funny to make your spouse laugh. You can wrap your arms around your spouse for a quick hug and say, "Long day but so glad you're home." In the morning, you can be the first one up and bring coffee to your spouse, especially if they usually make the coffee. Even if you are at odds with each other, you can choose to be kind. See—counterintuitive—not what everyone expects. We have a million little things we do when we first get married that override a million little irritations. Somehow, through the busyness of life and the passing of time, they fall away. It's not just about adding more things to your to-do list. It is, however, about getting a fresh perspective on your relationship and how a few tweaks that cultivate connection might begin to transform your marriage.

Over the last few years, I have talked to a few couples who feel that there is no hope for their relationship to change, that they are stuck in a lifeless or loveless marriage. So, they just go through the motions every day. My heart grieves every time I hear that because I don't believe God really wants that for us. I do believe we have to make daily choices to honor God in our marriage and seek His help to restore our relationships. I can't promise your marriage will become all you desire, but I can promise that you will change if you seek God first in this. Maybe you have been married forty years and feel like it is hopeless. What if it isn't?

Will change be difficult? Probably.

I don't know your situation. I only know that God gives hope and restoration. I expect you are afraid to hope because it might not turn out even if you do try. But if you don't try, how will you know? Some of you are going through very difficult situations. I don't want to make light of that for you. I cannot even begin to know where your journey has taken you. I only know that if you want to change your marriage, God is ready and waiting to help.

You just have to ask Him.

If you are not where you want to be in your relationship, you don't have to stay there. However, you do realize that if you keep doing what you have always done, nothing is going to change, right? What do you want your relationship to be like? I really want you to think about this next question.

What changes would you make in your relationship if you knew your efforts would not fail and the outcome would be a transformation in your marriage?

Although, instead of thinking about what you would like to change in your spouse, I ask you to consider what kind of marriage relationship you'd like to have and ask God to show you how to begin to get there. What changes are you willing to make in your relationship? Can you start by praying daily for your spouse and your marriage? Can you start by not complaining or reacting to a frustrating situation? Can you start by finding out your spouse's love language (I'll go into more detail on love languages in Chapter 14) and making a concerted effort to love them well? Do you need to start by setting aside time to talk or do something fun with your spouse? Dating is not a solution to marriage problems but having fun with your spouse can and will lighten the load you are bearing. It can build a bridge in your communication. It is a connecting point.

When relationships are strained by difficult circumstances, you *need* a connecting point, or you will just move further apart.

If you are struggling in your marriage relationship, chances are you are not connecting. Can you pray and ask God to show you where you might start connecting again? God knows where you need to begin and if you seek His wisdom, He will lead you. He says so in his Word: "If any of you lacks wisdom, you should ask God, who gives generously to all without finding fault, and it will be given to you. But when you ask, you must believe and not doubt, because the one who doubts is like a wave of the sea, blown and tossed by the wind." (James 1:5–6)

I believe in the power of prayer. I believe that we can ask God for a new vision for our marriages and then take the steps He lays on our hearts to get there. Remember, baby steps. Your marriage is not going to change overnight. It didn't get to the place it is overnight either. Your relationship is the by-product of hundreds of daily choices that you and your spouse have made over the years.

It is my experience that there will be things that come up in your relationship. There will be disagreements, differing opinions, and more, but we can't let them come between us. That's where we have to get on it already. If there is an issue that causes dissention then deal with it. Find a way to call a truce. Agree to disagree or get a referee! We've got to learn the win/win instead of win/lose philosophy. Can we both find a way to have the relationship we desire?

I really think we have to learn to fight *for* each other.

That includes what we take in through what we listen to, read, and even watch. There is so much coming at us day and night that is destructive. I mean, how many shows on TV and film are about people staying married? There are more affairs and divorce than ever before, and it is ALL over film and TV. I love a good movie, but my heart breaks every time a great romance is about an affair instead of honoring a married couple and their amazing adventure or triumph.

The King's Speech is a great film about Bertie overcoming his problem with stuttering and stepping into his role as king, but did you catch his marriage relationship? I delight that his wife, Elizabeth, loved him so deeply that she went to bat for him, took a risk, and did the unexpected because that is what it took. Then she embraced her husband every step of the way. Want a heroine? She was there for better or worse and helped him triumph over the difficulty. That relationship fed into such an amazing story! Every great marriage has a triumph somewhere along the way. There are more great marriage romance stories out there (take note filmmakers… you just have to look for them). It's not always about the burning desire for the one who got away.

How are we supposed to hang in there when everything in the media says marriage is dismal? The Ball and Chain? Now you have the "check in with the spouse" groan. My husband and I check in with each other out of mutual respect for one another. That's a good thing. My point is that there is plenty in your life to aid in tearing your relationship apart. Fill your life with positive affirmation of what you are going after to support your marriage along the way!

I actually turned to my friends for their input of movies that support a good marriage relationship. Here are a few examples in no specific order: *It's a Wonderful Life, Life is Beautiful, The Notebook, Fireproof, Date Night, Extraordinary, Ramona and Beezus, Father of the Bride, Shadowlands, Breathe, War Room, A Walk to Remember, The Case for Christ.*

I just recently watched *Breathe*. What a movie—and what a marriage! It's based on a true story. When this couple's life is drastically altered through disease, the wife champions her husband not only to stay alive but also to *live* to the best of his ability. It certainly was not the life either of them had planned. She was heroic in her love of her husband and family. It is truly remarkable what can happen in a marriage when *even just one spouse loves well* in the midst of really difficult life circumstances. Inspiring.

So how do we go the distance with our marriages? There are no easy answers.

In the pages ahead, you will read *our* stories of joy and struggle in marriage and those stories of the many couples that graciously let me into their trials and triumphs too. I am honored that these couples would share their stories with me. Some of whom I've known for years and some of whom I met throughout my research, but all of them were willing to be vulnerable for the sake of helping other couples, to share their struggles in the unexpected seasons of illness, grief, loss, infertility, infidelity, and addiction in their marriages. I think what you will see is that we all have difficulties: sometimes a lifetime of it. But God never said anything in life would be easy, He only said He would be with us through it all (see Matthew 28:20 and John 16:33).

I knew what had sustained us during difficult times, but I wanted to see what was working (or hadn't worked) for others. I spoke with both married and divorced couples to get their perspectives. I compiled all of it into my notes, but a few stories stood out that gave great insight.

These couples valued their relationship enough to press through impossible odds to get to longevity. Why? Because they believed in love and in the commitment that they made before God and their families, even when life was difficult. Over and over again there were similar strategies that kept coming up in each interview for those who went through hard circumstances and stayed together: revisiting commitment, leaning into faith and prayer, learning to communicate, extending forgiveness, cultivating community, practicing gratitude and celebration, and learning how to have fun with your spouse to build connection. Even while pressing through the hard stuff, it is these practices you will see that made all the difference in their journey.

My husband and I use them too.

Specifically, when life is stressful in our household, one of the things we do is turn to "fun" to lighten the load. My husband is the one who brings laughter and humor to our relationship and to our family life. His "humorous" is a good balance to my "serious" and I am thankful for that. When our children were small, and life felt frustrating, we would frequently put on music and have a "dance party" in the kitchen. Often, the trashcan became a drum set for our son and the slickness of the floor became a twirling ground for our daughter. It may seem silly, but it helped. Our emotions became lighter, and the music and silliness bred joy.

My husband and I still do that. Sometimes it is loud, fun music and sometimes it is soft and romantic as we dance around the kitchen floor. I love to dance. It is great exercise, but it is also a point of connection in our relationship. Notice, we don't have to talk. We can laugh together and dance together. You may not dance around your kitchen but maybe you cook together or garden together. Maybe you volunteer together. Maybe you ride bikes together. You can still do that when life is hard. I realize it is difficult to engage your spouse when you are going through hard seasons in life or your relationship. Habits we have cultivated together can sustain us at these times.

Finding connecting points with your spouse is a *discipline* you need if you want that relationship to last.

Again, it doesn't matter what you are doing as long as it is something that connects the two of you. My friend Anita says she and her husband ride a tractor around their property at night and watch the fireflies. Some couples sit on their front porch swing together. These things cultivate a sense of connection between them.

All of these stories are about staying connected through hard seasons in order to stay in love instead of allowing those circumstances to pull us apart.

That is what dancing in the kitchen is truly about.

Staying connected.

I hope you will see that. I hope you resonate with these stories and find ways to use these practices in your own relationship to stay connected in order to stay in love. In the days ahead, whether the music of your life is loud or soft, happy or sad, my deepest prayer is that you will learn to keep dancing in the kitchen for a lifetime.

Will You Dance

Lyrics and music by Debbie Cunningham

You walked into the room, took me by surprise
In just one moment my heart was mesmerized
Thought I was dreaming of words I long to hear
When you reached for my hand
Pulled me close to your side, whispered in my ear

(Chorus)
Will you dance with me
Can we learn to step together
and move across the floor
Will you dance with me
Not just tonight but forevermore

With each new song we'll learn to find the ebb and flow
And when the rhythm changes, be it fast or slow
We will find meaning in every melody
We'll spin and we'll twirl
Showing the world our love was meant to be

(Chorus)
Will you dance with me
Can we learn to step together
and move across the floor
Will you dance with me
Not just tonight but forevermore

(Bridge)
And when the music slowly starts to fade away
Will you go or will you stay… please stay

(Chorus again)
Will you dance… will you dance… will you dance

CHAPTER TWO
Art, Football, and Dancing

No, I've never thought of divorce in all these 35 years of marriage, but I did think of murder a few times.

—Ruth Bell Graham, when asked if she ever thought about divorcing her husband, evangelist Billy Graham[3]

The phrase "All you need is love" is everywhere in our culture, but how true is it? If all you need is feelings of love, then we are in trouble. When stressful situations arise with your spouse, feelings of love don't exactly pour forth. Most of the time when this phrase is used it is actually referring to deciding to love as a verb. Being kind, being compassionate, acting lovingly, even when you don't feel like it. That is what committed love looks like. In our culture we seem to confuse the two.

Romantic love is absolutely based on feeling. A kiss, a touch of the hand, the warmth of an embrace—these things send our body and mind over the edge with emotions. It affects all our senses. That comes in the beginning of a relationship. It is normal for the rush of those initial "feelings" to fade over time, but those feelings are seeds that can grow into a deeper, more satisfying reality if we cultivate it. How well do we actually communicate that in our society?

Choosing a spouse must move beyond "feeling in love" to "deciding" that this is a person with whom I can choose to build a life with over the years. This is someone who will be my best friend in good times and in bad. How do we build that kind of friendship in marriage? The same way we build it outside of marriage. We spend time together. We find common interests, and we do things together that we both enjoy. We cultivate a deeper understanding of one another, and we have each other's backs.

The difference in marriage is that there is a physical intimacy that brings that kind of friendship to a whole different level. And in friendship, don't we work out our differences? When we offend a friend, don't we strive to make things right or fix a misunderstanding? That decision will affect many other decisions we make over time too. For example, when we make a decision to take a new job, we do what that job requires. We don't run out the door as soon as the job requires more of us than expected. We learn, and we grow into that new position. A marriage commitment is no different in that regard, but it is more personal.

Spoiler alert: Marriage is going to require more of you than you or your spouse ever expected.

What about when we are angry? How do we love well then? First, we need to learn not to react explosively. It's important to try to see from your spouse's perspective as well as your own. This definitely took me a while in our marriage. Through the years, though, I learned to take my anger and frustration to God first instead of lashing out at my husband. Being reminded that we "all fall short of the glory of God" in our everyday lives is a good start. Daily experience in our marriage is opportunity for extending grace and forgiveness. However, that doesn't negate emotions or mean that "relational stuff" doesn't have to be dealt with. I think the hardest part of *any* relationship is learning how to deal with conflict. After all, God didn't say in Scripture do not be angry. He said, "In your anger do not sin." (Ephesians 4:26–27) And He also said, "Do not let the sun go down while you are still angry, and do not give the devil a foothold." From my understanding of the Scripture, its meaning is not so much that you resolve everything before sunset but that you start to deal with your anger right away and not let it simmer. Simmering and rehearsing the offense only creates an opportunity for a root of resentment to grow. That is a disaster waiting to happen.

I trust God to work in my relationship when I ask Him, and He always does. Maybe not the way I want, but He always works in us. God is for us, not against us.

His desire is for us to have a healthy marriage. I'm pretty honest with God in prayer too. I know he can handle my emotion and anger just as I handled it when my children used to overreact, and I waited patiently for them to vent. I knew that once the frustration was "vented," we could get down to the real issue of hurt or disappointment or fear. In those instances when I was frustrated or angry with Derek, I would pray. Actually, I would say to God in prayer (in a huff!) "God, *you* made him. I don't understand him, but you do. Please give me a heart to understand this man!"

I would think about whatever God impressed on my heart as I prayed about it, and my attitude would soften. It didn't mean I was wrong with what I felt, but I learned over the years not to react to those feelings. Whatever the argument was, we were usually both in the wrong at some level. We both wanted our own way. We had to learn to communicate and not react. I was the worst at reacting instead of communicating in the early days of our marriage. I am much better now but it took time, learning to lay down my attitude at God's feet and lots of prayer. Even now we keep working at our communication because even in the latter years of marriage, we can have huge bouts of misunderstanding. The truth is sometimes in conflict we are more concerned about changing our spouse rather than seeing the sin in ourselves, and God is more concerned about *transforming us* into HIS image individually as well as a couple. We are clay and *always* on the potter's wheel.

The quote at the beginning of the chapter by Ruth Graham is one of my favorites. Want to know why? Because Ruth was married to a wonderful man of God, the evangelist Reverend Billy Graham and even *she* felt frustrated enough with her own husband to say jokingly that murder crossed her mind a time or two!

Struggle in marriage is universal. Falling in love is easy… staying in love is hard. So how do we maintain it? What happens when we move from the season where love is so blind it overlooks all the idiosyncrasies in our spouse to the longer season where those same things begin to drive us nuts? We move from "feeling in love" to "committing to love." We move from dating to establishing a life together. Which means we have to communicate over everything, find compromise, pay bills, and maybe start a family too. It's really more about the middle season. I think when we move from feeling so in love with someone to needing to live in the commitment of that love, we panic a little. Where did the feelings go? Will I ever feel that way again? Did we make a mistake? What are we doing wrong? And my favorite: Is this normal? Does anyone else feel this way or just me? You know when life gets hard and the person you were head over heels about sometimes disappoints you. You didn't realize this is what you signed up for by the way, did you?

He loses his job and doesn't tell you. She overspent on credit cards and didn't tell you. She is not a good housekeeper. He works all the time. She is stressed out from raising the kids, and he's not paying bills. Romance is fizzling or maybe non-existent. You're sort of happy but not really happily-ever-after in the movies kind of happy because, now, there are these huge issues you are dealing with and more stress! Movies. Fairy tales. They speak to us and draw us in. We see the man tenderly and passionately kissing this woman he loves. He would die for her; she's so amazing. The woman is always beautiful, always strong; she always loves well it seems and would do anything for her man. Even in the story of Cinderella, this handsome prince is so captivated by a woman that he pursues her throughout the kingdom and rescues her from her drudgery, whisking her away to the castle. Who doesn't want that kind of passion and love? But then the story stops there!

We never see what happens behind the castle doors. It doesn't tell us how the two of them spent time together or learned to get along. Who made morning coffee? Who washed the dishes? Who was the better cook? Who made the money? Who paid the bills? Who stayed up at night when the kids were sick, did the grocery shopping, mowed the lawn, and how many arguments did they have when it came to in-laws, expectations, and sex? The truth is we all long for love that looks like the movies. Most of us never dreamed it could be as challenging as it sometimes is. Which of you does not want your spouse to love you unconditionally, forgive you, encourage you, and wrap their arms around you at the end of the day, say "I love you" and really mean it? So why do we lose it? What does it take to maintain a deep, satisfying affection for our spouse that lasts a lifetime?

In my own marriage, we've struggled just like you. We have a good relationship. We enjoy each other's company, have similar interests, and laugh a lot. However, we also disagree, get annoyed, and drive each other crazy some days! Which of course is normal. Over the years I've watched so many couples I know get divorced and it saddens me. I don't want to end up there; that's why I decided to research what it was that makes love last, especially through the hard seasons of marriage. When difficult situations arise, and we are weary of trying and not getting the results we want, how do we stay and fight instead of looking for greener grass somewhere else? (I promise you the grass isn't greener, they just water it more.) How do we get through those moments, so we can enjoy love again?

When we get married, we don't think about what is coming. We usually are present to all the wonderful things that falling in love brings. But what about those seasons when the vows we have taken rise to the surface through unforeseen circumstances? Did you mean... for better or worse, for richer or poorer, in sickness or health, to love and to cherish 'til death do us part? Allowing someone else into our own vulnerability is difficult and sometimes messy, as is stepping into another's with kindness. Brené Brown says in her book *Rising Strong*, "We can choose courage or we can choose comfort, but we can't have both. Not at the same time."[4]

I think in marriage we want comfort, we expect comfort, and when it gets UN-comfortable, we don't always know what to do.

We need courage. We need to be brave when things come out unexpectedly. It takes practice and forgiveness, and a kind of freedom most of us don't have when we are first going into a marriage.

I am a singer and a songwriter, but I enjoy the expression of art in many forms. From a very young age, I loved to draw and paint. I remember when I signed up to take my first art class. I was fairly good at painting and drawing but as soon as someone else had expectations of me, I froze. The freedom I once felt was gone and I couldn't create like I once did. I needed to find a method of practicing the new skills I would learn without losing the heart and joy that once came so easily in the beginning. Then I could apply those skills when tackling new and more difficult art assignments.

Marriage is similar. There is immense freedom when we first begin a relationship but as we progress, it takes courage when there are disagreements, disappointment of expectations, and difficult life events. It is easy to forget that people are imperfect. You are married to an imperfect person and so is your spouse. We need strategies to practice skills that once came so easily to get the results we desire. Instead of being filled with self-doubt and discouragement, we really need to remember that this is a normal part of becoming one throughout our lifetime of marriage. And it will change as the years go by.

Your marriage is a canvas, and everything you do and every experience you have together brushes color on that canvas. The resulting painting is a mixture of all of it. You might be thinking the portrait of your marriage is looking very bland at the moment, but you can continue to add color and use different brushes to get different effects as the years go by. You can make it brighter and bolder, but it is a process. You'll have to change your technique if you want the final product to change. If you are a perfectionist, like me, you will struggle with the freedom to make mistakes. I always have. The older I get, the more I realize that mistakes—and recovering or readjusting from them—hones our skills in a way that doing it perfectly the first time cannot. If you never have to work at it, you'll never get better at it. No matter what "it" is. The truth is we will never love our spouse perfectly, but we can get better at loving our spouse as our life together unfolds through the years. We will have wonderful seasons as well as seasons of heartache. No one is exempt. In the thirty years I have been married to my husband, we have found this to be true.

The beginning of my story, and experiencing results of hard seasons of marriage, starts when I was very young. I was born in Massachusetts, and we lived in Holyoke until I was seven years old. I had a five-year-old sister and a three-year-old twin brother and sister. I had just started the second grade when my entire life was uprooted as we moved unexpectedly from Massachusetts to Pennsylvania. We lived with my paternal grandparents while my parents were tirelessly looking for a rental house. Because it took a while, I had to start another school. Finally, a month later, we moved again. Unfortunately, our new house was in yet another school district. It was the third school in two months and thankfully the last one. This was a challenging transition for my seven-year-old self. Can you imagine? Life was already stressful just from moving. We lived in this new house a month when late one night I was awakened by someone yelling downstairs. It was my father screaming in a tirade, "I'm leaving and I'm not coming back!" He slammed the front door behind him and left. (I'm sure there are more details but that is how I remember it.) We didn't see him again for six months. Mom thought they would work things out. He wasn't willing. After that we didn't see him for five years.

So, divorce is in my history and, frankly, not a story I want to repeat. Not casting blame or bringing up details of their story, which is not mine to tell, just stating facts that affect my life and my marriage. My mom was an amazing anchor in our lives though. She handled raising four kids as a single parent with incredible grace. Fast forward to when I was fifteen, my mom married a wonderful man after dating him for three years. He proposed after three months! She was certain he had no idea what he was getting into, marrying a woman with four children. I'm sure he did not. However, after they got married he adopted all four of us and we became a family. I proudly call him Dad to this day because that is who he became to me. He and my mom have been married now for over thirty-five years. Currently, my husband and I have been married over thirty years. We are ALL learning this dance of staying in love, and it's a beautiful, messy process. We learn to master a few steps and then we stumble a bit, or so it seems. But every time I stand back and take in the progress of the life we are creating, I like it even more. It's an adventure. I believe that staying in love is a future and an adventure worth taking even if we do have to learn a thing or two.

A few years ago, I overheard a man say to his buddy in a grocery store, "Yeah, this pro-football season is getting a little like my marriage. I keep hoping it'll get better, but it never does." I felt annoyed. I was too shy back then to say anything to him. If I could talk to him today, first of all, I would tell him that *great marriages are possible,* but you can't sit on the bench and just hope the team gets better, you have to *do* something about it. In marriage, just as in football, both teams have to do the hard work of practice and building strategy in order to have a chance at winning the game! Paying attention when *your* team starts to fumble is crucial and training the players not to fumble next time is what will make the victory sweet.

It has been said that happiness is a journey, not a destination. The same can be said of a good marriage. It is a journey, and journeys travel over easy as well as rough terrain. In reality, you will have both. No need to freak out when that happens. It's

normal for all of us. I've never known a good marriage to not
have seasons of struggle. One of my pastors jokingly shared this
insight about struggle in marriage in his sermon:

**When you get married, you commit to becoming
one. Then you spend the next fifty years deciding
WHICH one!**

Fairly accurate, I'd say. That guy in the grocery store com-
pared marriage to football. I think marriage is a bit more like
dancing. It's supposed to be fun, but it is harder than it looks,
and it requires much practice and patience to get better. It takes
hundreds of hours to get *really* good and that includes mishaps
and bruises along the way. By the time you learn the steps to
one style of dance, the music changes and there is another dance
to learn, all while trying not to step on your partner's toes. As
you learn new styles, you will make many mistakes but that
doesn't mean you should stop trying. Perhaps though, you need
to stop occasionally, evaluate your approach, see what isn't
working, and try another technique to synchronize your move-
ments together. After all, this is a couple's dance and it requires
two people moving simultaneously. Most of the time, however,
one of you is much more skilled at dancing than the other. The
wonderful thing about this kind of dance, though, is that one
person can learn to *lead* their partner in the right direction even
if they miss a few steps. When you finally get to the point where
the two of you are gliding across the floor, moving at the right
pace and in the same direction, it can be the most exhilarating
experience you have ever known. Dance lessons anyone?

CHAPTER THREE
Matters of the Heart

*A cheerful heart is good medicine, but a crushed spirit
dries up the bones.*

—*Proverbs 17:22*

My husband, Derek, and I have experienced the need for cheerfulness to carry us through the hardness of life over and over in our marriage. Unfortunately, serious disease, financial troubles, job loss, and death can all be a part of our human experience. I remember one such season. It was mid-July 1998. I was about seven months pregnant with our son Drake and sitting at our daughter Deanna's three-year-old checkup. The appointment was routine, and we were just about finished when our pediatrician began asking me an unusual set of questions. "Have you noticed recently that Deanna tires easily?" Me: "No."

Doctor: "When she plays with other kids in the yard or at pre-school, is anyone noticing if she's keeping up with the other children or getting out of breath or stopping before everyone else?" Me: "No, not that I've noticed. The pre-school teacher hasn't said anything, but I can ask. When she plays with the neighbor's children she seems to keep up with everyone. Why do you ask?"

She pondered a minute and then said, "Deanna has a heart murmur. We've talked about that in the past, but it should have closed by now. It's probably nothing but a common murmur but *there's just something about the sound of it that bothers me*. I want to get her checked by a specialist." Dr. Fiscus, our pediatrician, wasn't an alarmist; I knew that, so I felt slightly concerned. She reiterated that it was probably just a normal murmur where she would have to be on antibiotics each time she had dental work done to protect her heart from bacteria, but she just wanted to be thorough and rule anything else out. So, we made an appointment at Vanderbilt Children's Hospital with the specialist she recommended.

It was August now and I was eight months along. I had also just started bed rest with this pregnancy, but nothing was going to stop me from going to this appointment. We arrived at Vanderbilt Children's Hospital for her tests. We were there for three hours. In that time, the EKG and other tests came back fine. Three interns listened and deemed it fine. The hardest part of the day was entertaining a three-year-old tired of being cooped up in this unusual setting. Then we met with Dr. Johns, the cardiologist. He had a kind demeanor, and we immediately felt at ease with him. He listened to Deanna's heart for what felt like a long length of time. He said, "I see that all the interns think it's just a normal murmur, and I think it probably is too, but *there's just something about the sound of it that bothers me*. Let's get a visual of her heart just to make sure before you leave. That way we can rule everything out."

We went into another room for the test. Fifteen minutes later he met with us again. "Actually, Mr. and Mrs. Cunningham, Deanna has an atrial septal defect (ASD) and she is going to need open-heart surgery. It is a necessity but not an emergency so let's get this new baby of yours born safely first. We will set up another appointment in six months to see how Deanna is doing and then we'll choose a surgery date in late spring or early summer. I want to be as far away from flu season as possible."

I felt like a lead weight had been dropped onto my chest; I couldn't breathe.

He discovered there was a hole in the upper chambers of her heart allowing oxygenated and non-oxygenated blood to mix. Eventually, she would not be able to live without this surgery. In fact, later we learned that we would be facing a heart and lung transplant in her teen years if we didn't have the surgery while she was young. The impending surgery and the wait through the coming months took its toll on our marriage. Any kind of waiting is difficult, and this waiting had uncertainty at the end of it. At first we comforted each other and expressed our concerns. We both processed our fears in our own way, and we needed each other differently.

I was a mess… getting no sleep with a newborn, trying to preserve every moment with our daughter and fearful of how many moments we had left with her. The prognosis was that she would most likely be fine, but the doctor and hospital personnel made sure we understood that there was a chance she could die. It didn't help that I had a few unexpected conversations with my three-year-old that left me questioning all that too.

Deanna did not know she was sick or needed surgery. The doctors were very clear to us that we should not discuss any of this with her until the day before the surgery to avoid inciting anxiety in her. As far as she was concerned, we just went to "checkups" with these doctors. She never questioned us. However, Deanna crawled up on my lap one day and said, "Mommy, I think I want to go live with Jesus for a while." I felt like my heart stopped. "Why would you say that?" I asked. "I don't know," she said, "I just would like to visit Him in heaven." So, I explained to her, "We can't *visit* Jesus like we visit Grandma and Grandpa or Nana and Pap-Pap. If you go to heaven to live with Jesus, you have to stay there, and you can't come back to live with Mommy and Daddy." "Oh, okay," she said. I held it together until I put both kids down for naps that day. Then I fell face down on my bed and sobbed uncontrollably. I didn't know where this was coming from. Was God preparing my heart to let go of her? Were they talking about heaven in Sunday school? That conversation stayed on my heart in the weeks and months ahead as we waited. This just added to the big emotional load I already had on my heart and when compounded with caring for a newborn, it was overwhelming.

I wanted to talk about being prepared for what might come and Derek didn't want to talk about it but needed to deal with it internally. I interpreted his lack of wanting to discuss this as emotional abandonment and I felt angry. At one very low moment I snapped at him, "Don't you even care what might happen?" A pained look came across his face like I had never seen. I wounded him deeply. I saw it in his eyes and heard it when he spoke, "I can't believe after all these years of marriage you would say that to me. Of course, I care! But I can't talk about it. That's not the way I process things. If I go there, I'm afraid the dam will break, and I won't recover. I'll cross that bridge *if* we come to it and not before." With one sentence of assumption and accusation, I hurled a knife into his heart. I apologized. He forgave me, but it took a long time to heal. **Men and women process emotions differently. We all know it, yet we seldom heed that knowledge.** However, that didn't negate the fact that I desperately needed someone to talk to about these things.

During difficult seasons, you must learn to find stress relief somehow or you will spew on each other. My girlfriends became crucial during this season to talk through my fears. I NEEDED to talk. My close friends were there to listen to the raw, unedited cries of my heart as I anticipated the impending surgery. Frequently, tears would come so unexpectedly no matter where I was. During one such occasion in the nursing room at church, I started to weep but quickly tried to stuff the emotions down. Fortunately, my friend Michele was there nursing her son too. She said, "Debbie, I can't begin to imagine all that you are going through emotionally as you face this. Please know you can vent your fears and frustration to me. I will not judge you. I am here to listen, and I will pray." There was so much freedom for me in that. I did feel under scrutiny of judgment from others if I wasn't handling this perfectly. I felt pressure to face this situation without doubt, to "count it all joy" and pretend I wasn't afraid. But I *was* afraid. I will ever be grateful for her words that day and her friendship. That conversation helped me not feel so alone and allowed me to walk through the rest of that season feeling whatever I felt without judging myself and trusting God with it as well. Just being heard helped me process my fears and allowed my relationship with Derek to be less burdened. He needed to process his own feelings, just not in the same way as I did. He needed space.

Having friends to walk alongside you as a couple without judgement in difficult seasons is not only smart, it is necessary. Our spouses cannot meet our every need. Only God can do that. But God also used our community of friends and intentional moments of humor as well as our faith to carry us through that hard season.

This is also a dangerous season in many marriages. We relied on our friends but so often when a situation like this arises, a spouse will seek comfort and understanding in the arms of the opposite sex. It's crucial for a couple to be aware of this and not go down that road. I've seen it happen many times. Friends need to be wise and encourage the couple in accountability with one another as well. BEWARE of spending time alone with a friend of the opposite sex. Too often a friendship becomes ripe for an affair when people are vulnerable. It is seldom intentional, but the enemy of your soul will seduce you quickly if you are not choosing wise boundaries in this season. As a friend, if we see this happening with someone, we need to speak up. Many a divorce has started this way. Trials either draw us closer together or push us apart. We need to be mindful of it.

In this season, I began reading Scripture and a devotional guide every day in the early morning feedings with my son. I had read devotional books on and off for years but now it was a necessity for me. Not because I am so spiritual, honestly, it was because I was so spent. Those moments with God were my very lifeline to sanity. Every day I breathed the same prayer during that season. "I am weary, Lord. I can't do this without you. Please carry me through." And He did.

We also stopped trying to put on a happy "Christian" front that everything was perfect, and we weren't worried about the outcome. We were anxious. And that was the beginning of our journey to truly learn what Philippians 4:6–7 really meant.

"Do not be anxious about anything, but in every situation, by prayer and petition, with thanksgiving, present your requests to God. And the peace of God, which transcends all understanding, will guard your hearts and your minds in Christ Jesus." (Philippians 4:6–7)

I sometimes had to pray hour by hour but, little by little, God's peace sustained us as we did what the Scripture said.

During that very stressful season, there were days when all we could do was get through the day. A friend shared with me on one of those long days that "Victory" sometimes looks like just not losing hope in Jesus through seasons like these.

I had a newborn and a three-year-old, and a heavy heart worried about the future. I barely had two to four hours of consecutive sleep because our son was also very sickly on top of everything else. I was at the end of myself and all I could do was rely on God for my very existence. That's it, and it was enough. I learned that He would carry me through as I relied on Him.

Derek was exhausted too! He was working forty to fifty hours a week. He was trying to care for our family financially, getting very little sleep with a newborn in our house and worried about the life of his daughter. We were both spent. We needed to learn to extend grace to each other. And we did. We knew this was a season and just purposed to forgive each other daily but it was difficult.

As tired as we were though, there was silliness and laughter too. We had learned to treasure that. The pressure I had felt on my chest the day of diagnosis continued through those months. I finally went to my own doctor for a heart checkup. Everything checked out fine, but he did prescribe one medicine: laughter and fun. He said, "I would be experiencing the same thing if my child had this diagnosis. I know it feels frivolous, but you and your husband *need* to find something fun you can do occasionally to release the stress in this season. See a comedian, watch a funny movie, get together with friends you enjoy… just do something. It's important for your sanity and your relationship." Thank you, Dr. Mike.

He was right. It did feel frivolous. How could I possibly have fun when it felt like my child's life hung in the balance? The truth is we all experience stress of some kind. Sometimes we just need to see a funny movie and laugh, dance in the kitchen with our kids or spouse, hang out with our best friends to let off a little steam, and chase those blues away. It's amazing how much it truly helps. Self-care is vital in the midst of the hard times. It'll carry you through… well, that and a whole lot of prayer. So, we made it a point to rent funny movies and have dinner with friends on occasion. It helped. We focused on enjoying the children too. Even when sick, children are resilient. Our daughter delighted in making her baby brother giggle. He delighted in his sister and that was soothing to our souls.

The night before the surgery I tossed and turned. I just kept praying, "God, please let this surgery heal our daughter and please let her be okay." The morning of the surgery, my mind felt like a video camera. As if I was recording every line of her face and hearing the sound of her voice, so sweet and so pure. It was embedding deeply in my brain. My neighbor came to watch our eight-month old son Drake. She hugged me tightly and said she was praying. I sat with Deanna in the back seat of our van to ride to the hospital. Truly I felt God's presence as we drove in the van. It felt like an invisible cloud around us all day long. So many friends were praying, and our church was praying too. We arrived at Vanderbilt Children's Hospital and they quickly prepped Deanna for surgery. Even though they handle a lot of serious children's illnesses, the staff is light-hearted and joyful. They know a cheerful heart is good medicine for everyone. The anesthesiologist blew up a blue rubber glove and gave it to her to hold. She was fascinated by it. His name was Dr. Oaks. As the drugs kicked in, she began singing silly songs. Then squealing with delight, she told us her doctor's name was "Dr. Oak TREEEEEEE!" It was hilarious. Laughter once again tempered the stress of the moment.

I'll tell you though, when there is nothing you can do but watch as your child is taken away on a surgical gurney, it is grueling. There is no magic wand.

Every false notion that we are in control of our lives, or even that we have the full ability to protect our children, crumbles in a moment like that.

The hospital staff told us, "You can go now." And just like that we felt alone. We knew my parents and a close friend were down on the first floor waiting for us. Our extended families and church friends were praying. However, all the people in the world couldn't change our deep feelings of powerlessness. So, we stumbled down the hall to the Chapel and we fell on our knees.

We knew we had no strength to make anything happen... only faith in the creator of the universe and the skill of a surgeon, and we prayed and wept together in our fear. We knew God could heal our little girl; we just didn't know what His plan was for her and we had to let go. I think that was the hardest moment in our lives as husband and wife. But we were in that moment together, weeping and praying. We both felt incredibly vulnerable, but we shared it. Not expecting anything of each other, just standing side by side. There is a depth of unity that takes place in our vulnerability when we share it with someone who receives it. This strengthened our relationship even though it was incredibly difficult at the time.

Over the next six hours, I felt like I couldn't breathe at times waiting for the updates from the nurse. Finally, the doctor wanted to see us. I never felt so sick to my stomach in my entire life. We didn't say much to each other but hand in hand got on the elevator to see the surgeon. I'll never forget how I felt when she told us our daughter had come through the surgery fine. I wept again but this time from relief. She wasn't completely out of the woods, but all went well over the next four days in the hospital and then the next month at home. Today, our daughter is living a normal healthy life. At her final follow-up appointment, when she was in high school, Deanna's cardiologist told her she was perfect. Trust me, she's sassy and never lets us forget those words!

We are thankful every day though that humor continues to be good medicine in our marriage and our family life. When we are anxious, we pray and trust because that is all we really can do. We incorporate fun and we rely on trusted friends when the going gets rough.

On a sweet side note: Our daughter Deanna married her high school sweetheart on the eighteenth anniversary of her open-heart surgery. It was doubly a day of rejoicing.

Practices for Staying in Love through Unexpected Circumstances:

—**Be intentional about friendships** before hard times come. Your marriage needs that. Remain in community with other couples who can encourage you when hard seasons visit. It is important to have friends who will hold you accountable and point you to God. This can lighten the load.

—**Laughter is good medicine.** This is not an easy "pill" to swallow when life is difficult, but you must utilize it. It helps. Try to laugh or find humor when you can. Enjoy the little things. Do something you enjoy.

—**Forgive daily.** When you are faced with an unexpected life event like heart surgery or trauma, everyone's nerves are frayed. Be kind and when you are not kind, be forgiving of yourself and others.

—**Honest, earnest prayer.** Just pour out your heart to God. He can handle it. He knows you are spent. No pretense needed. Just collapse there at His feet and ask Him to give you strength and wisdom. "Cast all your anxiety on Him because He cares for you." (1 Peter 5:7)

Do You Love Me

Lyrics and music by Debbie Cunningham

Do you love me
Will you love me forever
Take the time to ask
What lies behind the mask
Do you love me
Will you love me forever
Try to work things out
Don't get mad and pout

Do you love me
Will you love me when my hair turns to gray
When memory fades
Will you hold me
When laughter turns to tears
Oh, even then will you stay

Do you love me
Will you love me forever
Find a way to hear
When there's grief or fear
Do you love me
Will you love me forever
Through the trying days
When we lose our way

Do you love me
Will you love me when my hair turns to gray
When memory fades
Will you hold me
When laughter turns to tears
Oh, even then will you stay

I need you to love me that way
Oh, love me that way…

CHAPTER FOUR

Learning to Hear
through Grief

No one ever told me that grief felt so like fear.

—C.S. Lewis, *A Grief Observed*[5]

A t some moment in our lives we will experience grief. It may be over the death of a loved one or a job loss. It could be the ending of a season or the reality of an expectation that will never be fulfilled in the way you imagined for yourself. Loss plays a part in the landscape of living and no one escapes it.

Grief is predictable in that every single one of us will experience it in our lifetime. It is unpredictable, however, in when it will visit and how long it will stay.

The process of grieving is as unique as the person dealing with the loss. It requires courage and gentleness with yourself and your spouse. I wrote the song "Do You Love Me" after my husband and I had lost several family members and we were struggling in the aftermath of grief. Life was changing, and it was hard. I remember thinking that when we say "I do," we are totally in the moment. We aren't considering how age or time is going to affect our relationship. What if we lose our abilities or gain weight or lose our hair or our memory fades… will we love well then? And what about when fear shows up or people we love die and sadness abounds, can we find our way back to joy?

The first time my husband and I dealt with grief together was in 2001. My father-in-law had been sick for two years at this point. We scrambled to pack up our two kids and drive from our home in Tennessee to Pennsylvania to get there in time to see him the night before a second surgery. We had the most wonderful visit with him that night and, to this day, we see that time as a gift. He and my mother-in-law were delighted to see the children, and I will always remember the twinkle in his eye and the laughter our kids brought to him that night. He came through the surgery fine, and we thought all would be well. A few days later, however, he developed pneumonia and the doctor told us he was slipping away. We were able to be present with him when he died. All his adult children, their spouses, and his adult grandchildren were there with my mother-in-law by his side. We were sorrowful to say goodbye, but we sang worship songs and hymns in his room for an hour or so before he passed, ushering him into heaven. It was bittersweet yet a privilege to be there. We stayed for the funeral a week later. Actually, I really despise that word "funeral." It is so dismal. His service was a celebration of life! During the service, his kids, their spouses, and grandkids stood at the front of the church and sang his favorite hymn, "I'll Fly Away," and we honored the memory of the man known as Bill, Dad, and Pap-Pap. A delightful soul he was. Hard to let go of him but what a joy to celebrate a life well lived on earth. We then made the twelve-hour trip back to Tennessee.

After we returned home, our realtor informed us that our house had sold, and we had to pack up and move within a month. Talk about stress! The weariness of grief, no time to process the loss, caring for two young children, and packing up a house was quite a load. It was easy to be curt in our responses those days, but we did our best and forgave each other daily. We moved our belongings to storage and set up house in an apartment for five weeks while we waited for our new house to be finished. Our daughter started first grade and our temporary apartment was a minimum thirty-minute drive away from her new school. I tried to make apartment living an adventure. There was a pool and it was summer, so it felt like an extended vacation to the kids. I even wrote a fun bedtime song to sing to the kids during that season. They were in a strange, new environment, and it was always hard to get them to settle in for the night.

The Bedtime Song

Lyrics and music by Debbie Cunningham

Get in bed, close your eyes
It's time to go to sleep
Now's the time for resting
I don't want to hear a peep
(peep!)

Every time I sang it, one of the kids would gleefully sing that last peep! Giggles would abound, and we'd start again. But the laughter softened all the grief and change, so I welcomed it. Overall, this season was exhausting to Derek and me. All the extra driving to school or work and trying to find things in the few boxes we took there was frustrating. But we made the best of it.

Five weeks later, on Labor Day weekend 2001, we moved again, this time into our new home. It was the weekend before 9/11. With the crash of the twin towers in New York City, the whole world was definitely in flux. We were still processing our own personal grief and now there was this collective national grief to top it off. It took us months to get our bearings.

It was rough, but we learned in this season how important it was to seek to be *kind* instead of right on a daily basis.

About eight years later, grief ransacked our family again when my mother-in-law passed away quite suddenly. This time there was no warning, just a punch to the gut, or so it felt. We grieved yet celebrated again another life well lived to God's glory. Six months later, Derek's oldest sister, Debbie, had a stroke. Although we had been getting back to a sense of "normal," this tipped the cart a bit. The next nine months were spent in much uncertainty in regard to my sister-in-law's health. Then when she died it was difficult to get out from under the emotions of grief. We did celebrate her, another life well lived in service to Jesus, but it was much harder this time. Mostly because she was younger and had just begun to enjoy being a grandmother. We all felt she was gone too soon. The deaths were fifteen months apart.

We were spent. Our nerves were raw. There was little energy to say anything kind in those days. Derek and I we were not on the verge of divorce; however, we had quite a rough season in our relationship for the next few months. We were short-tempered and raised our voices over the smallest of things. It was extremely painful and at times it felt to me that our marriage was crumbling. I kept standing back and asking myself, "I deeply love my husband, why am I responding this way? I know he loves me but he's so angry all the time." I knew this had not been our normal mode of operation for most of our marriage, but it still felt scary. Our relationship felt so fragile in those days. That's when I realized that "grief" was talking.

I don't know about you but even though I said, "for better or for worse," I had nothing to measure it by. As I was praying about all of it and asking God for wisdom, it dawned on me one day that we were both still responding to the grief and fear we were processing. The two losses back to back took their toll on Derek, the kids, and me. As parents, we were trying to help our children cope, and we were so drained at times there wasn't much left to give to each other. In order to minimize long-term damage in our relationship, we needed to learn *how* to listen to one another in a different way. Unfortunately, I am not always a good listener.

Most people do not listen with the intent to understand;
they listen with the intent to reply.—

Stephen Covey[6]

When we listen without intent to understand where our spouse is coming from, our spouse does not feel heard or validated. It is very hurtful to a relationship and, if done repeatedly, can breed resentment. Men and women are truly complete opposites. Conversation to most women is one overlapping response after another with an occasional affirming nod. For most men, however, this can be perceived as incredibly disrespectful. Just as when men listen, they frequently say nothing.

When men say nothing, it is unclear to a woman if she is being heard or not. Women perceive this as being ignored or even worse, *invisible*.

Remember this: men and women listen and hear *differently*.

If you want to love your spouse well in this area, then make it a priority to listen to understand and not try to fix, reply, or interrupt. Ladies, many of us are terrible at interrupting. Just be aware of it. Occasionally, men, it is helpful if you indicate that you have heard us. Both of you must put down your phone and turn off the TV. You can take a drive or walk while you talk but looking at a screen is not only distracting, it's disrespectful. In hindsight, I wish we had gone through some grief counseling. It probably would have shortened our process, but we managed to muddle through by God's grace.

Through the years, I've experienced how important it is to choose love, kindness, and forgiveness every day... especially in the midst of hard seasons. Relationships are stressed in times of crisis. We need to be kind to one another. It takes patience and time to process the hard stuff. The words "I love you" are freely spoken when a new relationship brings the rush of emotions. However, love is more than a feeling. It is a verb.

True love does the hard work of fulfilling our vows as we go through the years together, even when we don't feel like it. It is not a one-time choice on your wedding day, but a daily decision to choose love as an action word.

"Love is patient and kind; love does not envy or boast; it is not arrogant or rude. It does not insist on its own way; it is not irritable or resentful; it does not rejoice at wrongdoing, but rejoices with the truth. Love bears all things, believes all things, hopes all things, endures all things." (1 Corinthians 13:4–7 ESV)

Life is good now, but will you love me through grief and sorrow? As we grow old and lose our abilities? When life is hard, and we feel lost in our relationship, will you love me then? Will you find a way to hear when I'm really struggling? It's not only what we are struggling with personally but as a couple. Aging parents to care for, kid stress, or losing a job can all be overwhelming and depleting. We need to care for one another and ourselves.

I've learned that answering those questions is a part of loving someone well. Every relationship has rough patches. In the practice of staying in love, we must find a way to help each other through those times. Grief can be overwhelming. It affects even the best of marriages and kids too. Be aware of that. There are stages of grief. It is a process, not a moment of working through sorrow. If you are struggling, there are lots of great books to help you process grief or seek out grief counseling. There is no shame in asking for help. We all need it from time to time.

Another sign that you need to listen differently is by observing how people behave. When we got married someone told us this: **"A bear growls when it is hungry."**

If your spouse is "growling," find out what they are hungry for and give that to them. Your attention or affection? Their personal space? A listening ear to vent sorrow or fear? Realize that sometimes your spouse needs you to listen and not try to fix the problem. Women, in general, need to *feel* heard. Reading the paper or checking your phone while she is sharing her day is not being attentive. It's amazing what five to ten minutes of facetime with your spouse can do for your relationship.

No one is irritable without a reason. If you can't figure it out, ASK! Sometimes we all just need food or rest. Life is exhausting at times. Ladies, if you are not being asked, please learn to ask for what you need. Don't be a martyr. It's neither healthy for your relationship nor attractive. Trying to get your husband to read your mind or pick up on hints will only frustrate both of you! Just ask for what you need. You'll both be happier. Be aware, too, when your husband is growling. He may just need quiet, a tranquil environment, or tenderness from you. It's give and take for both of you.

Practices for Staying in Love through Grief:

—**Listen with intent to understand.** Learn to listen/ hear what your spouse is communicating, verbally and non-verbally.

—**Patience and grace.** People dealing with loss need lots of grace. Extend it. If life seems unbearable, seek out grief counseling. It can help in the emotional processing and functionality of daily life.

—**Being aware of the seven stages of grief and what they may look like is helpful if you are processing a loss.** Shock, denial, anger, bargaining, depression, testing, and acceptance. That may look like a sense of numbness, then denial, emotional outbursts of anger or fear, disorganization, even panic, guilt, loneliness, and isolation. Depression can follow, struggling to find a new normal, finding new patterns then emerging to hope and acceptance. It is a process.

It can be overwhelming. It can come and go. If it becomes life-disrupting, however, seek counsel. It affects even the best of marriages and kids too. Be aware of that. The point here is that it is a process, not a moment of working through sorrow. If you are struggling, there are lots of great books to help you process grief or seek out grief counseling. There is no shame in asking for help. We all need it from time to time.

—**Give each other space to process emotions.** Don't stuff your emotions or they will come back with a vengeance later.

Day Like This

Lyrics and music by Debbie Cunningham

When the clouds come rolling in
And nothing is going right
Stress that is burnin'
Keeps you tossing and turnin'
All through the night
Pressure's mounting up
There are bills you have to pay
There's a time for deducin'
Finding solutions
But sometimes you have to play

On a day like this
We need to move, we need to sway
Lean into the wind
To blow all our troubles away
On a day like this
We need to dance beneath the moon
Sing a happy little tune
On a day like this

When the walls come closing in
And sanity's hard to find
Days are confusin'
And you feel like you're losin'
Your peace of mind
Tomorrow's looking bleak
Don't you give into those blues
Keepin' your eyes
Ahead on the prize
Remember you've got to choose

On a day like this
We need to move, we need to sway
Lean into the wind
To blow all our troubles away
On a day like this
We need to dance beneath the moon
Sing a happy little tune
On a day like this
You knew there would be days like this!

CHAPTER FIVE
Finding Hope in Loss

We must accept finite disappointment, but never lose infinite hope.

—Martin Luther King, Jr.

It was 2010, and our eyes were glued to the weather channel as the sound of the rain pounded against the windows. It had been pouring for forty-eight hours straight, and now there were two rivers forming in our backyard. Stressful thoughts began to race within my head. We didn't even live near a creek. How much more water could our little town take?

This storm had stalled over middle Tennessee and stayed too long. We were beginning to hear reports on social media that people were using canoes to rescue their neighbors just three miles from our house.

Twenty inches of rain fell in two days and flooded the streets. The city and surrounding areas were reeling from the mess it left behind. Whole neighborhoods were destroyed. There was mud and damage everywhere and sadly, as with most tragedies, a few people lost their lives. We did not have any property damage in our neighborhood because the flooding never reached our homes.

After the waters receded, my family and I set out to help those who were in need just a few miles down the road. We crawled under houses, pulled out ductwork, and hauled wet and muddy debris to trash piles on the curb. Others brought food and water. I remember feeling sick looking at a Corvette completely covered in mud, inside and out. The waters had been that high. I can only imagine the loss that car owner felt. But it caused me to think about the things in my own life that I cling to and value that can be taken away in a moment. Sobering. It makes you realize what is really important in those times: our relationships. Yet, there was so much physical loss to deal with for so many.

What we saw beside devastation, however, was this incredible spirit of community and gratitude that drew people together and began the process of healing. Whole neighborhoods of families who had never crossed paths before were meeting in central locations for food, water and connection. They all shared the same story, loss, and the same journey forward, rebuilding. As they continued to gather together, day after day, they began to smile and laugh together. There was music and moments of lightheartedness. We saw how community softened the hardship. Kids threw balls while parents chatted. What else could they do? By day they were cleaning up the mess, salvaging what they could, and putting their lives back together. In the evening, they gathered, shared meals under tents, played games... and that is where small, happy moments began to soften their experience; that and the hundreds of volunteers who showed up to care for them. I watched as couples laughed and cried together. There was loss.

It was stressful, and their nerves were frayed, but as they processed the loss in community, their load was lightened, and joy returned little by little.

It gave them strength to continue moving forward. I wrote the song that started this chapter—"Day Like This"—in reflection of what I saw during that flood. More importantly, to remind myself that we can't always stop the rain, but we can find a reason to dance anyway.

Living in community seems to be a forgotten art. In these days of social media friendship, electronic garage doors, and drive-through restaurants, we seldom have to physically connect with anyone. We have grocery delivery or pick-up services, lawn service, you name it—we can find it on the Internet. There are less and less chances to chat with our neighbor over the fence or run into them in the grocery store. Community is important when hard seasons come in your marriage. You need people who will pray for you, support, and encourage you as you go through each hard season.

I first met Sean and Jacqueline at a private event where I was the featured singer and entertainment. It was an evening of romantic jazz in the home of a friend of mine to *her community* of friends. I was presenting a house concert and speaking about my heart to encourage couples to stay in love through my album, *A Million Kisses*. I was quite taken with them as a couple. They were obviously very much in love. Throughout the night, during certain songs, she would reach for his hand as they listened. There was a gentle beauty about them. Afterward there was a meet and greet, and we got a chance to visit; I was fascinated by their story. He was quite confident and outspoken. She was also confident but much more reserved.

As I listened to them talk, I was intrigued by their camaraderie and how they worked together. They told me they met at Home Depot. She had just moved into an apartment and was looking for a few home improvement items, and he happened to be the employee who helped her. Coincidentally, she had just moved into his apartment complex. They crossed paths over the next few months and became acquainted, but it was quite some time until they actually started dating. In the first few years of their marriage, Sean was working in remodeling and using his GI Bill benefits to get a degree in accounting. He had always been good at numbers, and the plan was to be a CPA. At that time, Jacqueline worked as a bookkeeper for a property management company. Because Sean did remodeling work, her boss hired him as a vendor to do a little part-time maintenance on the properties. Through the course of some unexpected events, Jacqueline had the opportunity to become a managing partner in the company. The company was growing, doubling revenue, and it was quickly apparent they needed to hire a full-time maintenance manager and IT personnel. Sean had experience with both, so he was hired. Technically, his wife had now become his boss.

I asked him how he felt about having his wife as his boss. He laughed, "I learned quickly to check my ego at the door." Sean is extremely self-assured and confident in his abilities. Not one time, however, did I perceive that he had to prove himself to his wife or anyone else. In his perspective, he does what he is skilled to do and so does his wife, and that's where it all landed. In fact, a short time later her business partner passed away and she became the sole owner of the company. At that point, she asked him to consider a larger role. He made the decision to move into not only the maintenance manager but also into an advisory role for her since this company was now their live-lihood. So much for the CPA plans. But he had the degree in accounting and he was good with figures.

"She takes care of the daily and I'm always looking at the bottom-line financial reports saying where I think we can save money. I'm using my expertise in numbers, just not as a CPA. She is not always welcoming to change, however. It takes some convincing on my part. Even if I really know I'm right about something, I give her the facts and let her simmer with the information. I usually have to revisit it to get her to make a decision. Jacqueline can simmer over decisions for a v-e-r-y long time, but I want to get it done. Nevertheless, I've learned to leave my ego at the door of her office. It really doesn't matter that I'm her husband except for the trust factor there. She knows I'm looking out for our well-being as a couple and as a business. However, at the end of the day, she owns the company and she is the boss."

When I asked Jacqueline about how she felt about working like that with her husband, she said, "He's my partner in life. I trust him. We have different skill sets and I value and need his in the company. It doesn't matter that he is my husband. We learned early, though, not to take discussions personal, whether at work or at home. We call it debating." She smiled, "Sometimes people who work with us feel as if we are arguing but in truth, it is just a passionate debate. It is not always easy, however; we both have strong opinions. But we have a rule: nothing is personal.

"We established early that we are allowed to disagree on any issue, but that doesn't mean the other person is wrong or has done something wrong. We just see things differently.

"And we never assume that there is a hidden context to the discussion at hand. I think that makes it much easier to work together. And we really like spending time together. At this point, it's pretty much 24/7."

That doesn't mean their life together has been without struggle or disappointment. In fact, Sean's career goal to be a CPA was not the only dream that changed.

Part of Jacqueline's dream for her life was to have children. She had talked about it and planned for it for many years. They tried unsuccessfully to conceive for a very long time. They were both so disappointed. Then they decided to have tests done to see what the problem was.

Sean shared, "Imagine my surprise when I found out it was me who couldn't give my wife a child. I had male infertility. I couldn't believe it. I mean, I'm healthy and work out. She was heartbroken. She had this box with baby clothes in it that she had been gathering over the years and now she couldn't get pregnant. I honestly felt awful and like I was letting her down. Talk about dealing with my own ego. This was tough. First of all, I couldn't give my wife something she desperately wanted. She's the love of my life! Every day, I was the guy who found solutions to problems and fixed them. There was no fixing this, and it felt excruciating.

"Jacqueline and I have a deep faith, and we believe God can do anything. So, we prayed for healing and her conception. But He did not answer those prayers of healing for me. It was emotional for both of us. After a few months, she wanted to have discussions of other options for having a family. Adoption came up, but I wasn't sure how I felt about that. And Jacqueline *really* wanted to birth her own child. She asked me if I would consider in vitro fertilization (IVF). But of course, I couldn't supply the sperm, so I struggled with how I might feel being the father of a child who wasn't biologically mine even if it was biologically hers. I had a lot of emotions to work through regarding that. We just had to let things simmer a bit. It took some time, weeks actually, but I finally told her *yes* and we started the process.

"After the first try, Jacqueline got pregnant, and we finally felt excited. But then she had a miscarriage. It was so painful.

All our hopes at that point were dashed again. There were a lot of emotions we had to process about it all. We felt numb and disappointed, sadness, and anger too. All of it was so unexpected. Jackie got very quiet with her grief at one point, and we just didn't talk about it much. We both needed a lot of space. It was really our faith that carried us through that season of heartache and loss. Six months later, though, she wanted to try again. I was so unsure. I mean, I didn't want her to go through all that again and be crushed. We talked about it and prayed about it and ultimately, we made the decision to try one more time. She became pregnant again, this time with twins. There was trepidation, though, because of all we went through before."

Jacqueline said that even after miscarrying the first in vitro, as hard as it was, she still felt hopeful and just didn't want to give up at that point. Their hope finally turned into two beautiful babies, a boy and a girl. It was a long season of learning, disappointment, and testing of their faith and happened much differently than either one of them could have imagined. Ultimately, it was worth it.

I asked them how they stayed connected through all the disappointment of infertility, miscarriage, and of life being different than their initial plans. They said, "Our faith and our friends carried us and spurred us on when our sadness was overwhelming. Learning to not take ourselves too seriously and enjoy what we did have in the moment too. We had each other, and that is what we focused on."

Practices for Staying in Love through Loss and Disappointment:

—**Be honest with your emotions.** It's okay to grieve any loss. When you have a miscarriage, you still feel the loss of a child even if you never saw their face.

—**Embrace community.** Have friends you can be honest with and embrace the community of friends who can share your loss.

—**Lean into your faith.** Read Scripture that reminds you of who God is and that He is for you, not against you. Even though it feels differently in times of loss. Stand on truth.

—**Try to focus on what you do have that is positive.** It doesn't minimize the loss, but it helps in the healing process to have gratitude for what you do have.

CHAPTER SIX
No Plan B

...and he looked down at us—denying him, abandoning him, and betraying him—and in the greatest act of love in history, he STAYED. He said, "Father, forgive them, they don't know what they are doing." He loved us, not because we were lovely to him, but to make us lovely. That is why I am going to love my spouse. Speak to your heart like that, and then fulfill the promises you made on your wedding day.

—Timothy Keller[7]

When we get married, we are thrilled for the call to adventure, aren't we? We expect the best of one another or at least hope for it. We expect to build a life and to grow old together. Each of us has hopes and dreams of what that will look like. But what happens when serious illness, or even addiction, enters your relationship? How do you love your spouse well, let alone stay in love with them when serious illness comes into view? We seem to be able to muster the courage when our children are sick. We work together to help them get well. It's an entirely different situation when your spouse gets sick. If an illness progresses and years go by, it may demand more of you than expected. How do you walk that road?

My friends David and Tricia walked this journey. David told me one day, "I expected that in our eighties one of us would be following the other around with a bucket, but not at forty." David and Tricia were young when they met. David was seventeen and a senior in high school and Tricia was in college. When asked if they were dating, she would downright deny it. Three years later, though, at twenty and twenty-three, they were married. Tricia was a spitfire. From the first day I met her she had a twinkle of mischief in her eye and a great sense of humor. David was the worship leader at our church at the time and, since I sang on worship team, I saw Tricia often. Her sense of humor was one of the things I admired about her. Even when her disease put her in a wheelchair, she was still cracking jokes with that twinkle in her eye. David and I talked about their relationship before and after her diagnosis.

They were married in 1981 and had thirteen really happy years before Tricia was diagnosed with multiple sclerosis (MS) in 1994. They had a good marriage and a five-year-old. At first, the diagnosis didn't seem to impact their relationship other than trying to encourage one another through it. There was treatment available, and they were optimistic. Eighty percent of people with a diagnosis of MS will only experience a relapsing remittent version of the disease. Which means the symptoms would just come and go but not progress. Twenty percent experience a primary progressive form of MS. That's where you see the wheelchairs and gradual escalated debilitation. Unfortunately, within a few years it became clear that Tricia had the latter.

Marriage became an odd relationship with them as things progressed. The first few years after her diagnosis, the disease wasn't keeping them from doing things they wanted to do. Once things progressed, they stopped celebrating birthdays or anniversaries the way they used to because she couldn't go out or get out to buy a gift herself. (These were pre-Amazon days when you had to actually go to a store to buy a gift.) "We got take-out food and watched a movie to celebrate because that was all she could do. But that was fine." David said.

"Life wasn't turning out how we had hoped. We adjusted our expectations and just tried to focus on the things we *could* do instead of what we could not."

The relationship began to change though when Tricia had to depend on him for day-to-day things. She resented it, and he began to resent it too. "It became hard to distinguish resenting the disease from resenting one another. You resent the people you have to depend on. You just do."

He was angry and operating as a single parent. His wife couldn't drive because the disease was affecting her motor skills. She couldn't tell the brake from the floor, and he had to take her keys. That led to a lot of push back and forth—what the disease was doing to her and what she saw, his fears that she was permanently going downhill and losing quality of life. Soon, the pain of being a constant caregiver gave way to addiction for David.

A large percentage of people in caregiver roles end up in addictive behaviors of some kind. It might be alcohol, substance abuse, sex, food… whatever, but they turn to something as a self-medicating way of coping. In David's instance, he turned to alcohol and started drinking to cope. The sicker she became, the more he drank. The relationship changed because their roles changed. As her needs changed, her opinion of herself changed, and his opinion of himself changed. He realized he was in trouble when he started drinking every day to numb the pain. David explains, "I was hiding in plain sight. My personal life was one long stream of broken promises and my teenage daughter had lost all respect for me. My wife's eventually incapacitated state left me a virtual single parent who doubled as a nurse. My daughter had two sick parents. One whom she knew couldn't help it, and one whom she thought could. She was equally angry with both of us. I drank every single day for at least five years, and my life became a string of humiliating episodes that I constantly prayed would remain a secret from everyone in my ministry world. No one was more relieved than me when it all finally crashed." He sought help and got sober in 2005. Tricia passed away in 2013.

"The disease changed us. Now, as I do work with people in crises, I tell them all the time that Love will do what you cannot, but you have to adjust your expectations. If you think that as a caretaker you will be appreciated or validated in any way, that will never happen. Whether you are consumed with a need to self-medicate because of your pain or like Tricia, you are consumed by the fact that you feel betrayed by your own body, you cannot see the world around you. Everyone suffers in illness and addiction."

I asked David his thoughts on loving Tricia through her illness.

"Honestly, I knew she would have done it for me if it had been the other way around. If I had been the one in that bed, she wouldn't have had a second thought to taking care of me. Even as young and naïve as we were when we got married, we still stood in front of our family and our closest friends and promised God that we would take care of each other. We meant that. Even though I hated the disease and I hated what it did to her, I still in no way could imagine her going through that without me. There were days I didn't want to be there, and I would have taken a bus to anywhere but where I was at the moment, but I couldn't imagine Tricia trying to negotiate her own care just because I was over it. Who else was going to do that? Who else would I want to do that? Tricia trusted me. She didn't trust the whole world, she trusted *me*. I don't know where it fits in to commitment except we just didn't entertain Plan B... ever. We laughed and found the humor in the situation when we could. The humor was rooted in honesty and the surrealness of it all. Humor sustained us in a lot of ways.

"But the trauma of some of the things we experienced still has left its mark on me. No husband plans to see his wife with gaping wounds that have come apart after surgery or bones that are so contorted in a fall that are obviously broken. I still process some of that."

How did his faith play a part? He was baffled at first. He was a worship director at a large church in Franklin, Tennessee. He thought he was doing everything "right" so why this?

"Even now I don't understand the 'why' and I still don't like it, but I'm not raging at God anymore. It was helpful to me when I was able to turn a corner and realize that God was weeping and grieving WITH me in this, not doing it TO me and grading me on my handling of it. That's how I originally felt. Like I was going to have a lousy report card with God because I wasn't doing so well with all of it. And I couldn't square it with love either because I would never do this to my daughter. But a friend of mine who is a monk said to me, '**Until you experience Jesus grieving with you in this, you do not understand Jesus of the Bible. He is not doing this to you. You live in a broken, messed-up world where bad stuff happens.**'[8]

"I realized then that you are only going to be as healthy as the God you serve. If you are serving a God who is grading you, then you will deny your emotions in response to the situation. Anger, hurt, resentment, all of it. When you are able to admit it and see God grieving with you, walking with you, and providing what you need through it and all the things you can express gratitude for, then that gives you the permission to feel what you feel. That was my turning point."

He continued…

"I think it is easy to have an idealized notion of what a Christian who suffers should look like. I think if we are honest, we complain through most of it as most people do." David shared, "The caregiver is sometimes forgotten because the disease is the focus. But it's not just the patient but also the caregivers who are going through the trauma of the disease. This includes family members too. It can strain everyone. There is trauma that happens to you as a caregiver. And TRAUMA in the behavioral health world is defined as anything you experience that is painful or fearful when you don't have an empathetic voice speaking to you in it. And you don't know how to invite anyone into it either. It is healthy to get counsel early to help everyone cope." David had people around him who tried to help as Tricia's disease was obvious. Even so, it was hard to let them in at times. But what do we do with illnesses that aren't so visible?

Situations like a spouse with mental illness or obsessive-compulsive disorder (OCD) are much trickier to navigate. My friend Liz says, "I didn't know my husband had obsessive-compulsive disorder when we got married. It has progressed through the years. Different things trigger it. It is very hard. At times I've needed counseling to help me process and give me tools for coping. What keeps me staying in the relationship is my love for the man I married, my faith in God, and commitment to honor the covenant of marriage I made with him before God. It is difficult because it is an illness people don't readily see. My husband has worked on it through behavioral counseling, and that is brutal for him at times. He is suffering silently all the time, and I have compassion for him in that. I try to make life bearable for him without enabling him. I couldn't do it without my faith in God and my closest friends who pray for me regularly when I feel spent. We do have good times in our relationship too and I try to hold on to those moments. We try to build fun and laughter into our lives. I know my husband is trying and he loves me. It's not always about what makes me happy but what God is calling me to in this relationship. Yes, I'd like it to be easy. We are called to give God glory through our struggles, not just be delivered out of them. I do pray for healing for my husband daily, but it just hasn't come this side of heaven."

Practices for Staying in Love through Terminal Illness, Mental Illness, and Addiction:

—**Stay in community.** You need close friends who can hear and handle your raw, hard reality—who don't try to fix you or talk you out of how you feel, and you need to learn that it is okay to let people do things for you. There is no merit badge for doing it all yourself.

—**Self-care.** Get people to come in so you can go away. Caregiving is the most alienating, isolating, alone experience that someone can ever have.

—**Get counseling.** Caregivers frequently need counseling so that they don't fall into addiction, even though they think it won't happen to them. Be aware and get help when you need it.

—**Lean into your faith.** Realize God is weeping with you as you navigate hard circumstances in a broken world. He is not judging you on your performance.

—**Healing from addiction can be as stressful as remaining in addiction. Get the support you need.** "Many couples often move toward divorce in recovery than stay married in addiction because the roles they maintained in their marriage while in addiction were predictable to them. In the addiction, people know who they are and what to expect in their relationship (with their spouse), even if they hate it. In sobriety, the playing field gets plowed up. The sober person gets an opinion and finds a voice. All of this may threaten the person who has been carrying the load. If they are a person who needs to 'manage' people, it will be problematic in the relationship instead of a relief. People getting well is often as stressful as people staying in their abuse. Just be aware of that."—David Hampton[8]

Kiss and Make Up

Lyrics and music by Debbie Cunningham

Every couple once or twice
Has an exchange that is not so nice
Foolish are they who cling to spite
Wiser to be kind than right

So let's kiss and make up
Put a smile in our day
Live the life that we dreamed of
Instead of throwing that dream away

Life's too short to fuss and fight
I'd rather be in your arms to night
Silly pride, words in haste
Forgive me dear
As they say…

Let's kiss and make up
Put a smile in our day
Live the life that we dreamed of
Instead of throwing that dream away

CHAPTER SEVEN
Forgiveness Changes Everything

*Forgiveness is not a feeling; it is a commitment. It is a
choice to show mercy, not to hold the offense up against
the offender. Forgiveness is an expression of love.*

—*Gary Chapman*[9]

Grudges are devastating to a relationship. There's a saying that not forgiving someone is a poison you drink, hoping the other person will die. Holding a grudge just takes it to the next level of intensity. A grudge is something we cleave to when we need to be cleaving to one another. I read somewhere that trials become more difficult when we relive them over and over again in our thoughts. Sometimes we just lose perspective. Maybe because we've had a hard day, or we are stressed about other things. You come home after a long day and the house is in chaos; clothes are left on the floor, your spouse forgot something you specifically asked them to do or remember, then words are said in haste and, boom, we become enemies in seconds. We nurse those accidental wounds until they are full-grown assaults. And at those times, we are slow to forgive, especially if no one asks.

That is why I wrote the song, "Kiss and Make Up." It is a lighthearted swing tune that reminds me to lighten up a bit and let go of little offenses. If we don't learn to do that, we can destroy our relationship by holding grudges about things that really are small in comparison to the larger scheme of staying in love. We have to remember we are on the same side! We need to be at war *for* each other not *with* each other. Do we really want to throw away all we've worked through over the years, just to be right?

You may be thinking that you are always the one apologizing. Well, this is how I look at it. Ask yourself: If you or your spouse only had three months to live, would this bug you or would you let it slide? Usually, the stuff I'm talking about I'd let slide and you probably would too. When I ask myself that question, it softens my response because I focus on what's really important: my husband and our relationship. Because if one of you were that ill, you would be hyperaware of the fact that your spouse was off their game because of the illness. They are probably off their game because of their current stress load.

I'm not saying we don't need to work on the things that irritate each other but truly, it's so easy to get your perspective out of whack when life is busy and overwhelming. We all have pet peeves. One of mine is the apparent distance between the kitchen counter and the dishwasher! I really don't know why I get so irritated when I see the dish on the counter, but I just do. Maybe I feel disrespected in some way if I assume my family members are intentionally ignoring my request. (Assumption is my first mistake.) When I've shared my frustration, there is compliance for the most part, but I used to get so mad! When I finally realize my family just gets distracted and forgets sometimes, I can let it go. In fact, when I would call their attention to it their response was simply, "Oh yeah, sorry, I forgot. The phone rang, and I got distracted." It wasn't an intentional expectation that I am the maid. Although at times I may *feel* that way, it doesn't make it true. We have to pick our battles. Home should be a place where we can let that battleground go. Sometimes, however, the battle is fierce, and it is not such an easy thing to forgive an offense that deeply wounds the soul and cripples your relationship. How does one begin to forgive a life-altering offense?

My friends Jason and Penny have been married for thirty-eight years. Their story is a little more delicate in the area of forgiveness. They had some happy years early on. They struggled through infertility and then adopted a son. They enjoyed being parents and raising a family, even though it had been complicated at times. From the outside looking in, they seemed to be a perfect balance for each other. However, about twenty years into their relationship, they hit a long, rough patch in their marriage. They were both very involved with their church at the time. Penny said, **"We were typical, church going, comfortable Christians. We had never really needed to apply God's Word to see if it worked or not."**

Jason began the story, "One night, I sat on the bed praying to God for courage while Penny was in the bathroom. God, I can't tell her. It will crush her. I'm sorry for what I've done. I want to make it right, but if you want me to tell her, you're going to have to do it. I don't even know where to start." Penny had been praying too. She knew something was wrong in their relationship. They weren't connecting, and they were arguing and frustrated all the time. She asked God to show her what to do. The Lord spoke to her in her heart and said, "You don't know everything, and you need to ask him." So that night, she walked out of the bathroom, looked at Jason intently and said, "Did you have an affair?" Jason said, "Yes, six years ago."

Jason said, "It all began because I had been feeling convicted about the way I had treated a past girlfriend many years prior; I felt like I needed to apologize and ask for her forgiveness. One thing led to another, and I ended up committing adultery that same night. I should have never met with her alone."

The conviction was real… he had wronged this woman, but there is a reason Scripture says to flee sexual temptation. It seduces one like quicksand. "I should have safeguarded myself and taken a friend with me to hold me accountable. I knew it was wrong but then for six years I carried the affair in secret because I didn't want to hurt my wife by telling her the truth. I know that sounds stupid considering I had already done the damage by committing adultery in the first place. Because I was hiding my sin, it changed our relationship anyway, from that day forward. I realize now that I had started pushing her away, keeping her at a distance because I didn't want her to know the truth. The closer I felt to her, the harder it was to hide, so I did everything I could to keep her at arm's length. I thought if I made life miserable for us and she left me because of it, I'd have gotten what I deserved and not had to bare my soul to her. But she loved me through all of it. I didn't treat her kindly, and she just kept praying and loving and sticking it out. We argued, of course, but she didn't let that drive her away. I just felt guiltier and more convicted, but I didn't know how to handle it except to shut her out. God allowed life to get really bad in order for me to realize I had to deal with it. A week before we had that conversation in the bedroom, I had really dealt with God over my sin. I knew He had forgiven me and He was calling me to come clean with Penny, but I really didn't know how."

He continued, "I'd been sitting there on our bed asking God to help me to tell her and then she came out of the bathroom and asked me point-blank. In that moment, her heart broke and she began weeping. I had never seen her so hurt. Then something in me broke. I became undone knowing that I was the cause of all her pain."

His words were mixed with tears as he spoke to her then. "Penny, I am so sorry. I was wrong, and I'm willing to bear the consequences. It was six years ago and one night. I am truly sorry; I love you and I want us to stay together, but I realize this is your choice. Biblically, you have every right to divorce me, and I will accept that. Although I know I don't deserve it, if you forgive me and want to stay married, I want you to know I do love you and will do whatever it takes to show you I am truly repentant. It's completely up to you."

At that moment she looked at him and said, "You need to leave… as in, right now."

"So, I did. I called a friend to sleep on his couch. I gathered my things and made arrangements to live somewhere else for a while. I had been carrying this for six years but, to her, this had just happened, and she needed time and space to process. I told her I knew she needed moral support too, and she was free to tell my indiscretion to whomever she chose in order to get the support she needed, but I told her that I would tell her parents. I wanted to come clean with them. I had carried this sin too long, and I had ruined our life together. I wasn't going to put that on her. Her dad had given me his blessing to love, honor, and cherish her, and I had screwed it up."

Penny said to me, "He left. I sobbed and screamed to God. I was hurt and angry and every emotion in between. I had a physical pain in my chest that I had never felt before. It hurt so deeply, and nothing could take it away but time and God's healing. It was awful."

She told her closest friends and asked for prayer. Ultimately, she didn't know if they would stay married or not. Regardless, she knew she needed to forgive him because that's what God's Word says but it was going to take some time. "For if you forgive other people when they sin against you, your heavenly Father will also forgive you." (Matthew 6:14)

She had a core group of friends who seriously committed to praying for their healing and restoration and for God to sustain her. Initially, she didn't ask for healing of their marriage, just that God would help her process, forgive, and know how to move forward. She called a friend and researched legal things with her 401K for emergency withdrawals. She needed a plan. She was overwhelmed and deeply hurt.

During the next few days, one trusted friend bravely said something to her that stayed with her. The friend said, "As you are looking at options, remember this, whatever you decide right now will affect you and your son for the rest of your life. I know it may seem inappropriate for me to say this because of the pain you are feeling right now, but if you choose divorce in this moment, you are choosing for your son to spend every other holiday with you or your husband for the rest of his life too. Just consider not choosing hastily."

Penny said, "I didn't really want to hear it because I was so angry. But God was working in my heart too. I realized that I had a lot of issues to work on within our marriage besides my husband having an affair. Not that it was excusable. It wasn't, but I hadn't made it easy in our relationship either. I had a lot of expectations of my husband, and I put a lot of pressure on him to meet all my needs—needs only God could meet. God was opening my eyes to how that had affected our marriage over the years. I did keep thinking about how our choices would affect our son long-term. God used that and began to soften my heart towards the possibility of reconciliation. And I truly saw brokenness in my husband. He wept for four days... like you do in true grief. I saw he was not just grieving because he was caught but because he had hurt me so deeply. Seeing my sorrow somehow broke him. He was humbled and repentant."

They sought counseling and prayer and wrestled with God's truth in all of it. What did forgiveness and restoration look like after an affair? Was it even possible at this point? What did God require of them biblically?

After seeking God and searching her heart, she chose to move toward forgiving him. But that didn't make everything perfect again. She was willing to work on their marriage, but he had broken her trust and she didn't know if that could ever be restored. They began the hard work of rebuilding their marriage. The process to rebuild was long and arduous. They had started counseling together while they were separated. He moved in a month later. However, it was a long time before they were physically intimate again. They had weekly marriage counseling and homework for their relationship, which included a lot of reading books and discussing how they truly felt.

Penny shared this recently with me, "Before the affair, I was a typical, comfortable, Sunday church-going Christian. I was truly saved, but I didn't have the kind of faith that comes from applying God's Word to see if it was really a 'true after all' kind of authenticity. If this marriage was going to be healed, it could only come from God because I didn't have it in me to forgive and restore if God didn't do the work in me first. And God's Word made all the difference.

"The counselor was helpful to us too. He told Jason that if he was truly repentant, he had to be patient with me. 'You gave up the right to be indignant when you had the affair. If you are running late and she asks you where you have been, tell her. Be patient with her doubt and insecurities as God heals your trust with her. It will take a long time to restore.' He continues to be patient to this day. He knows it is normal to have moments of doubt when trust is broken. It is just part of the healing process."

Jason and Penny are dear friends of mine. To this day, I can see that they now have a wonderful relationship. I was one of those friends who fervently prayed and walked with them as they stumbled through the process of really submitting their relationship to God. I say "stumbled" because there is no manual for putting your relationship back together except that of applying God's truths and revisiting what a marriage is supposed to look like based on Scripture.

Jason truly loves and cherishes Penny as he never had before. I love to see them together now. They know how to find joy in little things, and they definitely know how to dance in the kitchen of life. They both praise God for the restoration of their relationship. When it was hard, though, they learned to lean in to putting on the armor of God in Ephesians 6:10–20 and believe God would battle their enemies. "Finally, be strong in the Lord and in His mighty power. Put on the full armor of God, so that you can take your stand against the devil's schemes." (Ephesians 6:10–11)

Ultimately, they know it is the enemy of their soul, the devil, seeking to destroy their marriage in the first place. They believed God every day and did the work of honest communication and working on issues and valuing each other. Penny says that she knew that deep communion with one another was missing in their relationship but now that is exactly what they have: a deep, satisfying communion with one another.

One of the things they learned through marriage counseling was that they needed eyeball time. Every day they "practice" by sitting on the couch together and talking about their day. Ten minutes to connect face to face has made all the difference in their relationship. AND they are honest. They talk about what they are feeling in their relationship instead of trying to brush it off or ignore it altogether, and they work on what is bothering them. It's not always easy. Nobody really desires dealing with conflict, but if you don't resolve small issues, they become huge in the end.

However, everything doesn't have to be an issue either. Penny said she also learned that she needed to lighten up and have fun with Jason more often. She was stressed and serious too much of the time. Shortly before their marriage fell apart, her friend Mary had mentioned to her in confidence that she was concerned about their relationship because she noted, "Those that play well together can easily fall into seduction." Mary had observed Jason playfully bantering with other women but not with Penny. Mary's advice to Penny was to try and lighten up and have fun with her husband. Now, she works to do just that. It is a practical safeguard in their marriage, and life is much more enjoyable.

When I asked Penny and Jason what it took to really rebuild their relationship they wanted to emphasize several things.

God did it. Once it fell apart, they submitted their relationship to God and asked Him to restore their marriage and to be glorified through it. They didn't really know exactly what that was going to look like. "If you have had a real encounter with Jesus, you'll know it. If you haven't really had to put His truths to the test, you don't really know if they'll hold water. Now we do."

They had friends fervently praying for God's will in their restoration. Penny said, "Remember in Acts 12:1–17 when Peter was bound in chains in the prison cell and the disciples were gathering and praying fervently for his release? Then in the middle of the prayer, Peter shows up and they think it is his ghost and that he must have died in that prison. They didn't even completely believe that God would do what they were asking him for! *My point is that God can work in spite of our imperfect faith!* We all have chains in our lives, from childhood experiences, sins committed against us, or choices we have made in seasons when we were not honoring God. We get used to walking around with the weight of our chains, and we don't pray to be set free, but they affect our marriages. Even when we do pray, we frequently don't completely believe it is possible. But all things are possible in Christ who strengthens us to carry out His truths and to bring Him glory with our lives."

Jesus even said in Mark 9:23, "Everything is possible for one who believes."

They got counseling and maintained accountability through the healing process.

They needed to learn to connect in a real way again as they had early on in their marriage. As they were starting over, they revisited their early dating and marriage life. "We were poor college kids when we first married, and we dated simply. We held hands and walked and dreamed together. We had forgotten to do that over the years. We found inexpensive things to do together that we both enjoyed. We spent time with friends as a couple too. We started there and really tried to talk and dream together again."

Practices for Staying in Love through Infidelity or to Safeguard Against it:

—**Get marriage counseling.** Don't wait for your world to crumble first. Be honest with yourself and your spouse if you are struggling in your marriage.

—**Have accountability.** Don't be alone with a member of the opposite sex, especially if you are struggling with an attraction or sexual temptation.

—**Practice facetime with your spouse.** Do this after one or both have had a few minutes to unwind after work. Try a ten-minute catch-up on the sofa to connect and communicate about your day.

—**Pray fervently and have friends who pray fervently for you.** If you are struggling, pray for God to heal your marriage. Believe that God will work on your behalf. When you struggle to pray in faith, ask for God to give you faith to believe and pray like the father of the demon-possessed boy in Mark 9:24, "I do believe; help me overcome my unbelief." When your "Peter" shows up released from chains, praise God for what He has done.

—**Have friends who will support you and keep you accountable.** No one does this alone.

—**Lighten up and have more fun with your spouse**—especially if you notice they are having fun with someone else.

**Debbie speaking—I am being intentional about having more fun with my husband. My family used to say I only had a serious side, and I needed to find my humorous side. Now they lightheartedly say, "Your serious is showing" and I know I need to lighten up a bit. I receive it instead of feeling insulted like I used to. After all, I'm a firstborn, a responsible planner-type, and I'm married to the youngest, carefree one. It's a process to balance both. In my family, they have to be a little more serious at times, and I have to lighten up at times. If you can learn to have a kind and fun way to express these things, it is like a little sugar that helps the medicine go down. Ask God to help you. He will. It's very important though for husbands and wives to have fun in their relationship.

—Journal through your process. Get honest with God. Penny said, "Journaling your honest emotions like screams, anger, and so on is crucial to getting it out of your head. Write like no one will ever read it and burn it if you need to but write what you honestly feel. Tell God. He is big enough to handle your screaming about the situation and when you have vented, then He can begin to work in your heart for healing."

Remember, God already knows what you think and feel. Trying to "hide" it from Him internally only harms your healing process, and it doesn't help your marriage either. Get real with God. He created your emotions and He can handle them. Even if you have been taught that He cannot. Trust Him to hear your true intentions. Once the explosive emotions are off your chest, He can get to the deeper areas and begin the work of healing your heart.

—Focus on God's Word. Apply God's truth to every situation and meditate on those truths when you can't shake doubt and fear.

A special note: If you have done all that you can do but your spouse chooses to abandon your marriage—please give yourself grace.

God gives all of us free will. Unfortunately, that means sometimes we reap the consequences of someone else's choices as well as our own. An acquaintance of mine shared that she wanted to save her marriage, but her husband did not. He kept having affairs. As a believer, she felt so much guilt that she could not restore her marriage. If you are in this situation, please understand you are not responsible for someone else's choices.

You both have responsibility to attend to your marital problems, but the one who responds by breaking the marriage covenant through adultery is responsible for that choice alone. It is not your fault. It is an issue of sin, their choices, and the seduction of the enemy.

Be kind to yourself and get the support you need to move forward after that. I encourage you to seek Godly counsel to help you process and restore your brokenness over the situation. As I have shared in previous stories, even marriages that have gone through adultery can be restored. But it requires both husband and wife being willing, accountable, and submitted to God for that to take place.

The righteous cry out, and the Lord hears them; He delivers them from all their troubles. The Lord is close to the brokenhearted and saves those who are crushed in spirit. The righteous may have many troubles, but the Lord delivers him from them all. **(Psalm 34:17–19)**

A special note to those struggling with shame if you are the one who had the affair:

I would be remiss if I didn't remind you that even though you have sinned and there are obvious consequences, God still loves you and forgives you!

Jesus died for our sin and once we are redeemed, we are a new creation. He casts our sin away "as far as the east is from the west." (Psalm 103:12) God is very clear in Scripture that His mercies are new every morning!

I remember my affliction and my wandering, the bitterness and the gall. I well remember them, and my soul is downcast within me. Yet to this I call to my mind and therefore I have hope: Because of the Lord's great love we are not consumed, for His compassions never fail. They are new every morning; great is your faithfulness. (Lamentations 3:19–23)

We need to go to God with our guilt and shame. We need to take the wounds we've received and the ones we've caused for He has redeemed it all. The death of Jesus on the cross has paid for all the sins we've physically committed and the ones we have rehearsed in our thoughts! Only God's mercy and grace can heal and restore any of it. Do not allow the enemy of your soul to entangle you again by insisting you cling to shame. Repent and seek his mercy. It is there to help you move forward in newness of life and bring you to dance again in the light of HIS love!

Here We Are

Lyrics and music by Debbie Cunningham

Here we are
You're still loving me
After all these years
It's still as sweet as it can be

Here we are
I'm still loving you
Nobody thought
We'd ever make it through
Yet here we are

I still hear music when you laugh
Feel sadness when you cry
I thought these days would pass
But they grow lovelier as time goes by

Here we are
Perfecting harmony
Obviously
We were meant to be
So here we are

CHAPTER EIGHT
A Marriage Arrangement

Marriage is a marriage—love or arranged. Both require the same level of commitment.

—Swati Kumar[10]

I was introduced to Saramma and John through a mutual friend. When I heard that they had an arranged marriage and were still married thirty-five years later, I jumped at the chance to interview them. The concept of an arranged marriage is foreign to our Western culture. We *fall in love* with someone romantically and try to make it work for thirty-five years. However, for these two people, their families chose them for each other.

Even more, John and Saramma are Christians. They both have fathers who were pastors in India, and it was so exciting to hear how the gospel has been a part of their culture and their families for generations. Because of John's mission work at a school in India, I was only able to interview Saramma. Their story is an amazing journey of God's faithfulness and their commitment that has produced great love in their marriage; I felt it an important story to tell. Before meeting Saramma, I knew very little about what an arranged marriage process actually looked like so that is where we will start.

For many cultures that still maintain arranged marriages, there has been an adaptation to more modernized thoughts around it. At one time, a bride and groom didn't meet each other until the wedding ceremony. (Okay, that thought alone fills me with great anxiety.) I'm sure it does and did for many women over the years. Every culture does not value women or women's rights so for most of us, this is an overwhelming thought. Saramma told me that although there is still much work to be done, there has been great improvement in her country in regard to this. There are females in government leadership and women accomplishing great things in India in a variety of vocations. I was eager to understand, however, how an arranged marriage might work in these modern times. She shared these thoughts with me.

An arranged marriage is more thought out than one might be led to believe. In her community, the families truly consider everything about the individual when trying to find a good match for their son or daughter. The parents and grandparents are involved frequently when looking for a possible spouse. Hair color, skin color, faith, personalities, family of origin, social and economic status, and political views are all taken into consideration in order to find a suitable match. It is a meticulous process, not a business arrangement as many Westerners have come to believe. The parents often go and visit the home of the would-be groom to meet him and his family to see if this would be a good paring. In some cases, this results in the father of the bride realizing the match would not work and so the search continues. There is frequently a dowry involved from the bride's family but not always. A dowry is an amount of money or estate property given by the bride's family to the groom and his family because the bride is joining their family. If there is a divorce, the dowry is supposed to be returned. In Saramma's situation, she was adamant that no dowry would be promised in this process if she were to consider an arranged marriage. So, there was not.

Saramma came to study in the United States when she was just fourteen years old. She finished her schooling and went on to college to get a degree in nursing at a Christian university. By the time she finished her degree, her parents had marriage prospects for her to consider. By now, however, she had been Westernized by our culture and wasn't so sure about this arranged marriage ideal. "I was starting to desire to fall in love with a knight in shining armor who would sweep me off my feet, as you say in America. But that wasn't happening." Still, she wanted to get married and honor her parents' tradition; she was the oldest and she was supposed to get married first. Her younger sisters were not to marry until she did, so that meant they were now waiting on her. The longer she waited meant the longer they had to wait, so she had a decision to make. Finally, she agreed, and the search began. Her family arranged a meeting here in America of one of the "prospects" who was living in New York at the time. After meeting, she didn't like him so that ended that. She noted that his ideals and aspirations were not the same as hers.

After that meeting, her cousin's husband asked if he could also look for a suitable spouse for her. She trusted her cousin and husband greatly, so she conceded. At the time, her cousin and husband were living in the United States but they happened to know that a pastor back in India was looking for a suitable wife for his son. Her cousin's husband thought Saramma would be a good match for him. The fathers of both John and Saramma began the process of getting to know one another to see if this would indeed be a suitable match. The fathers were both pastors, but they lived hours apart in India. They knew of each other but rarely crossed paths. It was the beginning of the families getting to know one another but *not John and Saramma.* Once the fathers approved that these two might be a suitable couple, John and Saramma exchanged photos but no letters or communication. "I really wanted to write to him and ask questions to get to know him, but we were requested not to per our customs. It was so hard, but I wanted to honor my parents. I just kept praying and fasting. I asked God if this was right for me and asked Him to give me wisdom if it was not."

It was decided then that Saramma and John would meet in India for the possible engagement. She made preparations to go to India for three weeks. "Before I left for India, I purchased a Bible and had John's name engraved on it as a wedding gift to him. I felt if he received it well, I would take it as a sign to say *yes* to the marriage." She also knew that once they met and she agreed to marry him, she would return in three weeks as his bride.

I kind of caught my breath for a minute. I just planned my daughter's wedding for an entire year! My checklist started running in my head: invitations, flowers, dress, decorations, and the food, oh my! Let alone the mental preparation for the couple. I can't imagine, my daughter getting engaged and married all within three weeks' time but that is their custom.

On February 4, she and her family gathered for a meal in their home with John and his family. The group ate and talked around the table for a long time. After the meal, Saramma and John requested a private space to talk with one another about the possibility of marriage. Saramma said, "We asked each other a lot of questions about faith and our expectations for the future. Including the question of where we would live. John was in law school in India and had been working in politics, and I had a really good job in Nashville at Saint Thomas West Hospital that I was planning to return to. He agreed to leave his political career in India and finish his education in the States. I gave him the Bible and he received it well. At the end of that time, about one-and-a-half-hours later, we emerged to tell our families that we had agreed to marry."

That began much preparation! There was to be an engagement service and dinner on February 10 and then the wedding service and celebration on February 17. The engagement in India is almost as big as the wedding. One family hosts the engagement and one family hosts the wedding. In this case, John's family wanted to host the wedding so Saramma's family hosted the engagement. And the engagement is a worship service similar to the wedding with a sit-down dinner like our modern receptions. It is a *big* deal. They are a week apart. Before that, however, personal invitations must be extended to family and close friends by personal visits to invite them. It is considered insulting if you do not receive a personal invitation unless you are too far away in another country, for example. So, the preparations began for both ceremonies and parties: the clothing, the food, and the decorations, all of it for both events.

The cities were several hours apart, so her family rented a bus for the whole extended family to travel to the wedding. She and her parents drove in a separate car, however. The bride and groom only saw each other two times between their first meeting and their wedding day. They were married on February 17, 1983.

"After the wedding, we do not go off by ourselves on a honeymoon either." Saramma said. "The married couple goes back and spends several days in one of our parent's homes. And we begin to adjust to married life." Then there was the immediate process of applying for John's visa to come back to the United States with her. But that was only the beginning.

The next year was difficult. As with any marriage, they adjusted to living life together as a couple. On top of that, John had to adjust to Western culture in America. He had struggles finding work. He had been in law school, was working in politics, and doing well in India but now he couldn't get a job. It was very difficult for him as it would be for anyone starting over. So much so that after one year of marriage and living in the States, John considered booking himself one plane ticket to go back to India permanently. Saramma said she just prayed and fasted and asked God to work in his heart not to leave. Their families prayed for them and their marriage too. So, he stayed in America and continued his studies but this time in business. Finally, he got a job. A short time later, however, he had a few health issues including a detached retina that affected his work, so he lost his job. That led to him starting his own company, which went very well but then the economy crashed, and the company folded. It seemed there was one discouragement after another.

"It was difficult adjusting to being married, being in a different country, now having financial troubles. We desired to have children but then we could not conceive. It was a very discouraging time. We had to keep praying and seeking God for help." Saramma said.

One practice that saved them was morning devotions. Saramma and John have morning devotions together every day before they go off to work. She credits her own father for instilling the discipline for being in the Scriptures daily from her upbringing. "When I was a child in India, my father would get us up every day at 4:00 a.m. to read the Scripture together and then do our school homework and studies. Of course, we didn't like it. We would never grumble about it to our parents, however, just to each other as siblings. But it instilled a discipline in me that has brought great reward in knowing God's Word. Even now we continue having devotions daily but not at 4:00 a.m.," she said with a smile. (I am a morning person, but I am with her on that one!)

Through all the hardship she and John had, Saramma kept praying. Their families were also encouraging them to stay together and kept praying for them. When I asked her if they ever considered divorce she said no, not seriously. It really wasn't an option in their culture. It was expected you marry for life. Although now, sadly, there are more divorces happening as Westernized thinking has affected their cultural traditions. **"In America, there is a lot of emphasis put on romantic love. But for us, although there is romantic love that can develop over time, the emphasis is on a commitment made before God and your family. It is not honorable to break that commitment."**

After many years of disappointment with a failed business, financial issues, and no children, John began doing some missionary work through his church. He had preached a few times back in India and it became apparent that he now was feeling called into a mission field. His father had started a college in India and John was returning frequently to work with him there and help grow that school. There were a lot of changes and travel, but they both felt at peace that this is what God was calling them to. And to this day, that is what John does. He is in and out of the country. Saramma joins him in India when she can, but she still maintains her job as an ICU nurse in Nashville.

When I asked her if John had any comments in regard to their marriage and what makes it possible to stay together, she said, "I asked John what he wanted to share in regard to this and this is what he said, 'Tell them: keeping our commitment and God's grace to us.'" Saramma concurs. They are incredibly happy and thankful to have each other now, but she says there were years that were very, very hard. They could not have made it this far without the prayer support and encouragement of their families and God's strength to keep their commitment to one another.

One wife of an arranged marriage told me: **"In the West, you marry the one you love. Here, we love the one we marry."**— Shared by Pastor Mike Smith

Practices for Staying in Love through an Arranged Marriage:

—**Prayer and fasting.** Saramma prayed for wisdom and sought God to help her honor her family's culture and customs. She asked God to choose a spouse for her through this process. She credits God for holding them together through hard seasons.

—**Lean into faith and commitment.** When life circumstances were difficult over the years, she and John stayed in their commitment to one another because they believed in the covenant they made before God and their family. They sought encouragement through studying God's Word together.

—**Embrace the doors that open when your expectations do not materialize.** She wanted to fall in love first, but it didn't happen. Yet she has a loving marriage now. She and John wanted children but never could have them. His business failed and then the ministry doors seemed to open for him. They had much loss, but they kept seeking God's plan for their life.

—**Support from family and friends is crucial.** She trusted in the care her family gave for finding her a spouse and their prayer support and encouragement when the relationship hit hard seasons as all marriages do. John did the same.

—**Cultivate your relationship.** Every marriage takes commitment and choosing to "love" your spouse as a verb, whether that relationship started with an arrangement or a romantic love. Feelings of love are cultivated through loving actions.

Do What Lovers Do

Lyrics and music by Debbie Cunningham

Seems that we forget what it was like
When it was just you and me
Get so busy with the house and our jobs
Now we have a family

When that family is up and grown
It'll just be you and me baby, all alone
So let's dim the lights to a softer hue
And do what lovers do

Kiss me sweet, hold me tight
Wrap your arms around me all through the night
Pull me closer when we dance
We can't forget the romance

Don't need money or a paradise
Being with you is perfectly nice
Let's just remember our whole life through
To do what lovers do

CHAPTER NINE

The Roommate Dilemma

Romance is the spice that makes your marriage more than just being roommates.

—*Laura Beckder*[11]

In the Oxford English Dictionary, romance is defined as a feeling of mystery or excitement, and remoteness from everyday life associated with love. Isn't that true that it feels that way when you fall in love? I really like that they included the phrase "remoteness from everyday life."

I think that *is* what romance is supposed to do. In a sense, it is to *whisk* us away to a moment for just the two of us, away from everyday living.

It's not really a card or a gift as much as it is creating a moment with a card, a date, a special dinner, or just unexpected thoughtfulness. The focus is on the relationship between the two. It binds us together by setting us apart. Might I also say that romance looks different to each couple. Only the two of you can create what whisks you away from everyday life. It can be a walk in the moonlight, an unexpected embrace, a date, or a trip. It may be a walk in the woods or sitting on the patio watching the sunset, bringing your wife flowers, or cooking your husband's favorite meal. It's not any one thing. Ahh… but it is another connecting point in your relationship.

Often, once married we seem to stop cultivating those romantic moments. But why? Perhaps if it was part of the wooing of love during your dating days, it may feel as if it is not necessary anymore. That couldn't be further from the truth. I don't know a married woman alive who doesn't want to be whisked away, do you? And ladies, our husbands appreciate a little romancing too. It just may look a little differently than ours. I think we get complacent in our marriages. In my song, "Do What Lovers Do," I address that we need to be intentional about romance even after we are married. The busyness of life, jobs, and caring for families can drain us dry. If we forget about cultivating love and romance together, when the kids leave, or we retire from our jobs, what will be left of our relationship?

Lisa and Kenneth are a lovely couple I recently met. Lisa is a colleague of mine in the Christian Women in Media Association. She is always very positive about her relationship with her husband, Kenneth, but it wasn't always that way. They just celebrated their thirtieth wedding anniversary with a renewing of their vows. I was so intrigued by all the "gushing" I saw as she spoke about it that I asked Lisa to tell me more about their journey as husband and wife.

Lisa was introduced to Kenneth at a birthday party for one of Lisa's relatives when she was in high school. Quickly, they became friends for a season and then started dating. This was Lisa's senior year. She was making plans to attend college and Kenneth was going into the Air Force. Not long after they started dating, however, Lisa's mom committed suicide. Even though this was young love, Kenneth was by her side through all of the emotions and grief that come with such a traumatic circumstance, and he quickly became her rock. She knew this was a man she could depend on. They began to talk about marriage.

By the time Kenneth went to boot camp, however, Lisa found out she was pregnant. So, they did get married just a little sooner than they had planned. Now Lisa's college plans were on hold, and they were moving to Kenneth's first assignment in Texas. Thus, they began their married journey with a move away from their home state of Indiana and everything that was familiar.

New state. New marriage. New baby.

It wasn't easy, but they were committed to figuring it out as they went along. They learned to be married and be parents as they matured as a couple. They enjoyed travelling with each new assignment. It was an adventure. Japan was first. Kenneth loved it there. Lisa did not. The real struggles began a few years later into their marriage when they were reassigned to Germany. They loved Germany: the people, the culture, all of it. But this quickly developed into the season of major job stress for both of them. Lisa had a job in management at the military childcare center. She was also in volunteer leadership at their local church.

She loved the work she was doing at church. She was thriving and spending lots of hours after her traditional nine-to-five serving the congregation there at least four days a week.

Although she loved the work, there was additional stress of being in the leadership too.

At that same time, Kenneth's job also became very stressful, and it was not a job he was enjoying at all. Over the next two-and-a-half-years, the pressure began to mount and grow like a snowball rolling down a hill. Just to add fuel to the fire, their son had now become a teenager and was struggling with a little bit of rebellion.

Because of their schedules, they hadn't spent much time together since they had moved to Germany. They became distant. They were not communicating.

They weren't discussing their teenage son's issues together as a couple or as a family. Their son was spending time with one parent or the other but rarely at the same time. They weren't even communicating about their stress at work. They began to live very individual lives at this point. Kenneth was becoming more and more angry and resentful that she was spending so many hours away from the family. When he would make comments to her, she would try to justify her time away, saying that she was doing good work at the church. Then she would feel resentful to him because the church was work that she loved and fulfilled her. At one point, she even said, "Well, if you want to come and spend more time at church, you are welcome to come and engage more with me there."

Their teenage son was going through teenage defiance and was experiencing independence during this time, which wasn't always very beneficial to him.

They started snapping and being unkind to one other and then began separating themselves from each other at home. Of course, this "emotional separation" affected their physical intimacy too. When they were home together they would frequently be in different rooms.

Both of them were stressed and tired with nothing to give to each other.

Kenneth finally broke the silence one day and said, "This is getting old. I'm tired of it. Maybe our marriage isn't going to work. I don't need a roommate."

That was the turning point. They began to look at what the problems were. They were both working too many overtime hours. He was serious. Life had to change, or they were done. Kenneth started leaving work on time except for the occasional day when it was required of him. They instituted a weekly date night too. He even shared this with his boss. He was a First Sergeant Superintendent, and he worked for a Commander. He explained to the Commander that this was important to his marriage and, unless it was absolutely necessary, he needed to leave on time on Fridays. When his boss would request a meeting on Friday nights at 6:00 p.m., he would smile and say, "Okay, we can meet but you know this is my date night." If his boss said, "We really need to have this meeting," Kenneth would first make a phone call to let Lisa know he'd be late and why. If it wasn't absolutely imperative, the meeting often waited.

Lisa had to cut back her volunteer hours and leadership at the church. Kenneth said, "The fact was her position there was not paying the bills. The number of hours she was spending there was also negatively affecting our quality of life together and as a family." It wasn't the church itself, but that Lisa spent so much time there. Lisa admits now that this was hard for her, and it felt very sacrificial at the time because she loved the ministry work at the church so much. However, she knew in her heart that it was out of balance. She also had to make some adjustments at work. Instead of staying after closing hours and doing paperwork, she learned to leave at closing time and go home to her family. She realized she hadn't really been paying attention to her husband or her son. **"God was always my number one, but he gave me my husband and son before he gave me my position at the church. I realized I had to prioritize my family. God didn't want me serving to the loss of my marriage. I had to set many new boundaries."**

They started communicating more and taking weekend trips with each other and their son. It made all the difference in their marriage and their family life. Things began to get much better. Even after they left Germany, however, they were struggling with communication, so they had to keep working at it. Lisa can be very independent, which was helpful when Kenneth was deployed. Not so much when he returned home. This definitely can be an issue for many couples when one spouse travels for business. You are always adjusting to living as a couple one minute versus as a single individual the week.

For Lisa, it was months at a time that she was responsible for everything and operating as a single parent. Then the spouse comes home, and everything has to change. It is a difficulty in many military families. It definitely requires grace and patience. Changing their communication habits was not a quick fix, but they kept working at it. Instituting a weekly date night truly helped. Kenneth shared that he loved date night once they started it. Surprisingly, Lisa initially felt like it was just one more thing on her to-do list. She said, **"Honestly, date night wasn't always easy at first, but we made the commitment to go out and do something together even when we didn't feel like it, and it made all the difference."**

They have now been empty nesters for ten years. They still keep their weekly date night, and they both look forward to it now.

Also, during that two-and-a-half-year time span, Lisa was dealing with past issues. She said, "Funny, as a believer I just wanted God to 'fix' my husband. But He said, 'No, I'm going to deal with you first.' God began to show me that my mother's suicide had impacted me far greater than I had ever admitted. I did grieve some, but I was immediately thrown into becoming a wife and a mother, so I moved on quickly. Later in this season, as we were working on our relationship, I began to see symptoms of PTSD that I had not dealt with as God was really dealing with these things in me. I knew I was struggling but, initially, I didn't really allow Kenneth into that struggle with me." There were lots of misunderstandings, but they kept working at it. Instead of arguing when discussions got heated, they would stop and walk away to cool off. The problem was they didn't come back and try to resolve the issue later.

They would just let it go. Kenneth shared that was a really frustrating thing to him when disagreements didn't actually get resolved. Issues just got left in the silence. Which is another thing that built their emotional wall of distance.

Now, however, they resolve things differently. Kenneth said, "Even now there are times when Lisa doesn't want to talk about something. However, I just say okay, you don't have to talk about it, but I need you to hear what I have to say because it is bothering me. You can answer it or not. She can let it settle in or whatever she needs and then I'm good because I've gotten to say what I needed to say." I laughed because they are so opposite of my husband and me. I'm the one who needs to talk and be heard, and Derek is more like Lisa. Lisa said that was an adjustment for her because she isn't as much of a communicator in conflict. She could just drop it, move on, and it was over.

It's really not a male vs. female thing as much as it is a personality difference. There are many couples who are like this but often traditions and society assume it is the other way around. We are byproducts of our upbringing, and we have to address how those things affect us in our marriage relationship through the years. Initially, Kenneth was very quiet but over time he became a communicator. Lisa was an only child and was used to making a lot of decisions on her own. They had to learn to express their likes and dislikes with one another in a kind way and not in the middle of conflict. You have to be in a good place to have a serious conversation. When you don't say something and then stew over it in your heart, that's not healthy because then one day you blow up inappropriately. Over time you have to figure out what you can let go that isn't going to fester. We have to choose our battles wisely. Everything can't be a huge issue.

Recently, Kenneth and Lisa celebrated their thirtieth wedding anniversary. When they got married, they were in the midst of a huge transition with the recent death of her mom and a baby on the way. At that time, they just had a house ceremony with a pastor, a stepmom, and an uncle—not even their parents. They never really took the opportunity to have the wedding they would have liked. Reflecting back on all the years of struggle and how they had matured gave them such joy. They knew it was because of God's help and their commitment to each other that they made it through, and now they really wanted to celebrate their marriage and milestone with their families. So, they planned a week in Las Vegas including a vow renewal ceremony and reception with twenty family members and a few close friends. They even exchanged their original wedding rings. As they reflected back over the years of struggle, they rejoiced in all that God had done for them to get them where they are now: enjoying the fruit of all their relational labor.

Practices for Staying in Love When You Have Become Roommates:

—**Communicate.** We all can have compounded stress in our lives, including our children. We have to find ways to communicate in a healthy manner. If something is not working, stop and reassess. If it means sitting at the dinner table and talking over a meal, or pillow talk, we have to take the time. As parents, we also have to realize our kids, especially our teens, also have stress, and we need to give them an outlet to communicate that to us without penalty.

—**Critically listen.** In communication, you also have to learn not just to talk but also to listen and not always respond. One spouse may always want to fix. Sometimes a person just needs to be heard.

—**Embrace vulnerability.** You need to be vulnerable, not just strong with one another. If you are struggling, you need to find a way to be honest and communicate what you need. Kenneth said as a military guy he struggled with it but realized he had to communicate to Lisa that he was stressed about the job and their marriage. Being honest about that wasn't a sign of weakness but the beginning of their road to recovery and healing.

—**Have faith.** Lean on your faith in God to help you make and keep the commitment you made to one another. Ask and trust God to help you adjust your priorities and make the necessary changes needed to have a healthy relationship.

—**Date your spouse.** Make dating your spouse a priority. They don't have to be expensive. It's really important to find time to "connect" with your spouse outside of the day-to-day existence.

CHAPTER TEN

When Suffering Persists

Although the world is full of suffering, it is full also of the overcoming of it.

—Helen Keller

My husband and I have been friends with Mark and Melanie for many decades. We actually met at a church outside of Philadelphia where my husband was the choir director. It was one of his first jobs after graduating college with his music education degree. We were all in our twenties then and shared a love of music together. I have truly watched them endure a multitude of suffering over thirty-three years of marriage. However, their relationship through all of that has grown more lovely and strong with God's grace and a beauty that is deeply rooted in commitment and learning to love each other well. It hasn't been an easy journey though.

Their story began at seventeen and nineteen when they met. They dated and then they were married two years later. By 1992, they had two young children, good friends, a church they were involved in, and life was pleasant. At this point, they had only been married eight years when things started unraveling with Melanie's adoptive parents. "My mother was mentally ill. She had been verbally abusing me for years and had continued to do so. Mark and I had many conversations about how I should handle this. On one occasion, I finally stood up to her. Mark also intervened to protect me. Instead of opening a dialogue, my parents chose never to speak to me again. It's called 'emotional cut-off' and even though our relationship was unhealthy, it was devastating. Especially because I had always been very close to my father and he allowed my mom to shut the door on our relationship as well. We were estranged for twenty-five years."

Melanie was adopted so in her mind she had already been rejected once and now she was being rejected again. The complicated grief sent her into a spiral of PTSD over the next year. She developed an eating disorder and suffered from depression. By 1993, however, she realized she needed outside help and began her healing journey through counseling. She knew Mark couldn't fix her problems, and she didn't ask. She leaned on her faith in God to process the grief, and she took responsibility to get well by seeking out the therapy she needed. "It was a long, painful process because I had grown up with my mother's mental illness. I could never measure up to her expectations. She constantly criticized and belittled me. Now, as an adult, I knew that it was her issue not mine, but as a child, I was just trying to please my mother and couldn't understand why it seemed that she hated me." In therapy, she began to unpack the baggage of all the unhealthy coping mechanisms she learned in her family of origin.

"We all have learned ways of coping from our upbringing. In marriage, we have to be patient with each other when those learned behaviors clash," Melanie said.

"Mark was my rock. He supported me through my trauma and grief recovery for years. It was a very long process." When I asked Mark about that season, he said. "It's easy to look at your spouse and think, 'Can't you just hurry up and get better?' But you have to be patient. You have to try and understand what that other person is going through. People have different ways of processing their emotions, and you can't demand they do it your way. It takes time. You have to let people feel the way they feel and love them through it."

It took several years of therapy, but life was changing for the better. In 2001, Melanie had the opportunity to reunite with her two sisters from her birth family. Her birth mother had passed away by then, but the sisters were able to share that they had all been trying to find Melanie for a long time. The only reason her biological mother had given her up for adoption was because she couldn't afford to take care of her. Over the next few years, the sisters became a part of her family's life and God brought much healing through that season. By this time, Melanie had not only raised two children but also emerged from the dark season of the earlier trauma. She had gone back to school and earned her degree as a licensed clinical social worker. She wanted to help others the way she had been helped. She opened her practice in 2004.

However, from 2005–2008, a whole new season of difficult life circumstances washed over their family for a few solid years. Mark said this next season was the hardest for him. So many losses through death came back to back. Mark's sister died unexpectedly from alcoholism in 2005, and Mark and Melanie became legal guardians of her youngest child in addition to their two at home. Melanie's oldest birth sister then died in

2006. That same year, their daughter's serious boyfriend was diagnosed with cancer, and he died in February of 2008. "That season was really hard on our marriage. To watch your daughter watch the love of her life die was so difficult. Our hearts were breaking because her heart was breaking. There was family grief, too, over his death and our daughter's loss of hopes and dreams for the future. It was really hard, especially for her." A few months later, in May, Melanie's other birth sister committed suicide. This was also another painful loss. After being reunited with them and finding new joys, now both of her sisters were gone too. Literally, they were just getting through each day the best they could to survive.

Less than three months later, Melanie was walking for exercise as she frequently did and out of the blue, she had a grand mal seizure. She had never had a seizure before, and this was new terrain. She attributes staying alive to God's grace too. "It was strange that day. I was about to go back home, which was quite far, and I felt the strong need for a glass of water. My best friend, Phyllis, lived in that block, so I stopped by her house to get water and get out of the heat for a minute. When Phyllis returned to the living room with the water, I was already having the seizure. I know God prompted me to go there or I probably wouldn't be alive."

They couldn't seem to get out from under the onslaught of grief or trials that year. One after another they came. They were overloaded on so many levels. The stress began to show up in their relationship. "There were times I wanted to talk to Mark to process my own feelings of grief and frustration, and he didn't want to talk. Because, as I've come to learn, that is how he processes. Many times, it made me angry. I felt like I was falling apart, and he was silent. I read his lack of emotion to be that he didn't care. I felt emotionally abandoned. We did start couples counseling to help. We both had to learn to give a bit.

"Our communication patterns had been deeply established by this point in our marriage. I pursued him, and he retreated. The harder I pursued, the more he retreated. Mark had learned to be silent and not respond when he was growing up. When there was anxiety or frustration in his home, everyone stopped talking about it and just moved on." Because Melanie's adoptive mother used this as a control mechanism, it triggered her feelings of emotional abandonment. When her mom was mad at her dad, she would go days without speaking to him.

"Even though I am a therapist, I am still learning to give Mark more space and time to process his feelings before asking for a response. He's getting better at letting me know where he is emotionally and not being completely silent when we are dealing with something too, which helps. We knew during that season that it was important to get help to stay healthy in our marriage. Because I've worked with so many couples, I know that when the storms come, they just sink. They project their pain and anger onto each other and sink into addictions of all kinds: pornography, drugs, infidelity, workaholism, etc." She continued, "**It has been difficult at times, but we have learned to endure suffering with patience and build our house on a firm foundation with God's help. We personally have always strived to love each other based on God's definition in 1 Corinthians 13. But it is not always easy.**"

Over the last several years, another heartache re-opened as Melanie got a call one day that her adopted brother had died. "The hospital called me and asked me to notify my parents. I was listed as the next of kin. It was really difficult to have to re-enter that situation. I called them to let them know and that was it. A few months later, my dad called to tell me that my mother was very ill and asked me if I could come by the house. I prayed about it a lot. I really wasn't sure if I could open that door again, but part of me wanted to be there for my dad. Mark cautioned me as he had seen what this had done to me before, but he was again supportive of my decision to go. It was really emotionally painful. But God's grace was pouring out on me in a new way. When I went in, I spoke to my dad and went to sit by my mother's bedside. It was a pitiful sight. How weak and frail she had become. Seeing how the years had aged them took me by surprise. In my mind, they were as they had been when they closed the door on our relationship because of stubbornness and pride.

"A lot of things came flooding in, especially all the things they missed with our children. My mother looked up at me sitting there and said, 'You used to come here.'

"'Yes, I did. A long time ago.' I managed to whisper.

"Her voice was faint and weak, 'I think I was mean to you. I'm sorry.'"

Melanie continued, "I knew at that moment I had to forgive her. It was so hard though. She had robbed me of years with my dad. But I prayed under my breath for God to give me strength to forgive."

God brought new healing to Melanie that day. Life is still difficult at times, but Mark and Melanie embrace each trial by leaning on their faith and each other to carry them through the hard seasons.

One of the things they shared that truly helped them cope and strengthen their marriage was establishing regular date nights.

Just having one-on-one time to connect has solidified their relationship and helped build that firm foundation.

They are grateful to be in a new season now that they are enjoying their empty-nest years. Through her practice, Melanie is helping other couples find hope and healing in their seasons of suffering. They are both thankful that God is bringing encouragement to others from all the years of trial they endured.

Practices for Staying in Love and Strengthening Marriage through Suffering:

Since Melanie is a licensed counselor, I asked her to share her thoughts on this.

Build your House on the Rock: Matthew 7:24–25 (ESV) says, "Everyone then who hears these words of mine and does them will be like a wise man who built his house on the rock. And the rain fell, and the floods came, and the winds blew and beat on that house, but it did not fall, because it had been founded on the rock." The verse goes on to explain how a house built on sinking sand will fall. If you're married, you already know that the rain will come and at times the floods will come too. A marriage that weathers the trials of life is built upon a firm foundation, the rock that is Jesus Christ. What does this look like? It requires two people to be in agreement in their faith beliefs and practices. Worshipping together, praying together, growing in God's Word together.

Pray for Hedge of Protection around Your Marriage: In the Bible, we see different accounts where walls are erected to protect cities and gates as the only way to enter those cities and to keep the enemies out. At the gates are guards. These walls are built as a hedge of protection. Who you allow inside the walls of your marriage is very important. Remember what Scripture says in 1 Peter 5:8, "Be alert and of sober mind. Your enemy the devil prowls around like a roaring lion looking for someone to devour." I believe that the enemy is on the prowl for our families, and he wants to devour the covenant of marriage. I tell my clients that they must build a hedge of protection around their marriage and even discuss what that would look like. Where do boundaries need to be set with co-workers, family members, even church family? As a family, what are you allowing you and your family to consume on TV, social media, and other outlets? If you have friends of the opposite sex, are they also friends with your spouse?

Intentionally Nurture the Relationship: As married couples, we must tend to our relationship with one another just as we would tend to a garden. It must be watered and fed; the weeds cannot be allowed to grow around the healthy soil and foliage. Date your spouse! Be intentional and choose one day a week as date night. Have fun! My husband and I are now empty-nesters, and we have discovered our love for playing video games together. It gives us a time to laugh and be playful with one another. We will also play board games too. We are sure to plan at least two trips a year with one another. You can plan a day trip, a weekend trip, or a full week. Leave sweet notes for your spouse, text during your day and just say, "I love you" and "I'm praying for you." Do not become complacent and take the relationship for granted. Within that hedge of protection is a beautiful garden that must be nurtured.

—**Melanie M. Eddy MSW, LCSW,**
Encourage Her Christian Coaching and Counseling, http://encouragehercoachingandcounseling.com

CHAPTER ELEVEN
Marriage and the Empty Nest

Should we take up a hobby together, so we can stay
connected next year when the kids are gone?

—Elizabeth McCord, Madam Secretary (CBS)

I think Elizabeth echoes the fear that many couples feel as they approach empty nest. How will we stay connected now when so much of our relationship has revolved around our kids? Even in my good relationship with my husband, I have faced those moments of struggle to connect. Funny, my original outline for this book did not have an empty nest chapter. I didn't see it then as a possible hard circumstance in marriage. However, this took me much longer to write than I had originally anticipated. I suppose our son's senior year, high school graduation, college applications, seven trips for college auditions, and our daughter's college senior year, college graduation, planning and celebrating her wedding, as well as recording and producing my second album all in the span of the last twelve months of writing had something to do with that. WHEW!

However, because of the delay, I have also entered this new season of marriage called the empty nest, which has given me yet another perspective to shape my ideas of what it takes to stay in love. It is a difficult yet beautiful thing: this process of letting go of your kids as they traverse the world on their own. All the time I spent prioritizing their well-being over my own actually smacked me in the face when our son left for college. It is not as if I didn't know what I was going to do with my time. I now had ample time to grow my music and speaking career, performance coaching, and work on my writing. But WOW! I was so sad, and I felt so lost.

I really underestimated how much grief I would feel. To me, it was strange because I was so happy for my kids and where their lives were taking them. Our son was thrilled to be accepted into a great BFA program that was preparing him for his performing aspirations. (Never mind that it was ten hours' drive away from home.) My daughter was happily married to her high school sweetheart, now Airman, husband. They moved away and were off to start their own adventures in life and another state—and I heartily endorse "leaving and cleaving" to your spouse! I was happy for both my kids. However, it all happened in the same year and I felt overwhelmed when the motion of it all suddenly came to a screeching halt.

I wept… often. I said to my husband, "I knew I'd be sad, and I'm so happy to have this time with you, but I can't stop crying lately about all the change." He said, "Well, technically, you just lost a job you loved and have had for twenty-two years. Give yourself a little grace." I realized it did feel a little like being let go or downsized, and even though I saw it coming, it still hurt. This is what we've been waiting for though, isn't it? Finally, the freedom to go and do as we once did when we first became husband and wife. A season where there are less demands and more spontaneity. Yet for some, this is a frightening prospect. All of a sudden, there are no children to occupy your time and immediate attention, and a new normal must emerge. Cooking once again for two and schedules not full of PTO meetings, school sporting events, choir concerts, and theater performances. There is no carpool schedule or chauffeuring children around.

Exciting or terrifying?

It depends on what you have cultivated as you approached this season.

If you have been invested in family life to the neglect of your marriage, this can be a tricky transition.

This season can expose gaping holes in your marriage relationship that were easy to dismiss before because your *focus* was on raising your kids.

Struggles in marriage start long before the big argument. Just the stress of everyday living is enough sometimes to really tip the cart. It can sneak up on you too. Even if you think you have been attending to your marriage, you can wake up to a dry season emotionally when the kids leave. What then? In seasons of distress, we need to be aware of traps we can fall into as a result of our own fragility. When we are weary or wounded, it is easy to lash out at those closest to us. Problem is when we are both grieving a loss or going through a stressful season, it's not as easy to rebound because we are both in the same broken state. If we are not cautious, we can do great harm to one another. In their book *Guide to the Empty Nest*, Barbara Rainey and Susan Yates warn couples about three pitfalls they can fall into as they are transitioning to the empty nest years, and I believe it is pertinent to marriages in all seasons:

1. A critical spirit

2. Emotional divorce

3. An affair

All of these are worth our consideration because the first two lead to the third quite often. When you are weary, it is easy to cooperate with a critical spirit. Have you ever noticed that the accusations seem to come out of nowhere? Your spouse walks through the door and you are immediately irritated by anything he or she does. It is almost like those cartoons when someone is in the middle of a dilemma and the little angel and devil appear on each shoulder beckoning the character to make their side of choice. The cartoon devil downplays the consequences and the cartoon angel just tries to get you to do the right thing. A lot of relational disaster could be avoided if we hushed the voices in our heads and paid attention to what God says is the right course of action. The truth is we have an enemy constantly accusing us and those we love. Your spouse is not your enemy. There is a battle in our minds, and we have to get a handle on it or it will affect our relationships

Ephesians 6: 11–18 says, "Put on the full armor of God, so that you can take your stand against the devil's schemes. For our struggle is not against flesh and blood, but against the rulers, against the authorities, against the powers of this dark world and against the spiritual forces of evil in the heavenly realms. Therefore, put on the full armor of God, so that when the day of evil comes, you may be able to stand your ground, and after you have done everything, to stand. Stand firm then, with the belt of truth buckled around your waist, with the breastplate of righteousness in place, and with your feet fitted with the readiness that comes from the gospel of peace. In addition to all this, take up the shield of faith, with which you can extinguish all the flaming arrows of the evil one. Take the helmet of salvation and the sword of the Spirit, which is the Word of God. AND PRAY in the Spirit on all occasions with all kinds of prayers and requests. With this in mind, be alert and always keep on praying for all the Lord's people."

You know, just this one verse could keep us busy for a lifetime if we really applied these things to our marriage battles. We need to remind ourselves of the truth in God's Word, remember we have an enemy to our marriage (and it is not your husband or wife), live out the gospel of grace to our hearts daily by extending forgiveness and mercy to our spouse! Isn't it easy to extend mercy to everyone *but* our spouse? It seems to be that way for me some days.

Now let's talk about those critical attitudes. It helps me to add a little humor to the mix when dealing with them. I name them. Literally, I have started giving them names like Critical Callie. I thank Critical Callie for pointing out the obvious and tell her she isn't needed because Gracious Gwen is going to lead the charge on this one. I know it sounds silly, but it is fascinating to me how detaching the personal aspect of my attitude and adding a little humor goes a long way in giving those voices and attitudes less power. It allows me to laugh in the moment and let it go. I have Perfectionist Polly (in my life she's the worst!), Fearful Francine, and so on. You get the picture.

We all have them—attitudes, spirits, whatever you want to call 'em, we got 'em and they rear their ugliness in our marriages. If you are constantly critical, it can really drive a wedge in your relationship, and that wedge will turn into a wall if you don't deal with it. If you ignore those things, they become a barrier. Eventually this isolation can lead to emotional divorce if you don't recognize what is happening and make the choice to *not* be pulled away from your spouse. So many marriages today exist in emotional divorce even if they don't move to a physical divorce. It is heartbreaking to watch two people once very much in love crumble like this.

They stop being connected and no one says anything; they just feed the negative hurts and the distance grows like a wild fire. If you find yourself in this state it is really important to discuss this with your spouse and probably seek advice with a licensed counselor, pastor, or a wise couple. SILENCE WILL ONLY EXACERBATE THE PROBLEM. Silently choosing to forgive someone is completely different than silently stoking the fire on emotional wounds and distance. If you don't address it, you will give the enemy of your soul a foothold.

> **"Failing to stop the drift toward emotional divorce makes us increasingly vulnerable to an affair."**
>
> **—Barbara Rainey and Susan Yates**[12]

The transition to empty nest can be fun, but it can also be lonely, especially if all your friends were parents of your kids' friends. Women most especially fear and feel a loss of connection in relationships at this time. When the last child leaves, she may feel stressed over losing the connection with her children and friends she doesn't see anymore because their friendship was through school activities. Husbands and wives may not know how to maintain connection with each other either if much of their "connection" revolved around their children. This can be a huge source of stress in a marriage relationship. Extend each other grace. You will need to build new friendships with couples in your same stage of life. Many friendships grow around proximity. Because of school activities, parents gravitate toward each other, but if there isn't an intentional cultivation of those relationships outside of school activities, the friendship will die as the activities cease. The wonderful thing about empty nest is it actually gives you a brand new canvas for your marriage and the next phase of your life together. Even if you realize it hasn't been all you wanted, you can commit to changing it now. What do you want it to look like when you finish life? That's what you should commit to working on now as a couple.

Invest in a new definition of romance.

This can also be a really wonderful time for self-growth too. Are there classes you have wanted to take or a language you have wanted to learn? Are there dreams for yourself that you put on hold while raising a family? How about that anniversary trip you and your spouse always dreamed of taking? This is a fresh new season to do those things!

Practices for Staying in Love through Empty Nest Years:

—**Grieve the ending of an era.** Then embrace a new season of adventure for you and your spouse.

—**Start dating your spouse again.** Find new hobbies or things you can do to enjoy your time together if you don't already have this in your life. Be adventurous! Cultivate things you think may be fun to continue doing as you age too.

—**Be intentional about cultivating friendships of couples in the same stage.** Cultivate a new community. Chances are many of your friends were the parents of your kid's friends. You were together because your kids were together. Many couples find themselves longing for friendship in this season and dealing with a strange sense of loneliness when the kids leave. Perhaps you could join a small group at church or start a hobby together.

—**Lean in to your faith and pray for God to lead you in this new season.** Prayer is essential in all seasons. Either seeking God's wisdom or giving praise and gratitude for what God has done in your life. Living this way is a discipline worth pursuing.

—**Have courage.** If you realize you and your spouse are not really connecting, just begin now to take steps toward that again.

—**Make a bucket list together** and start planning to do some of those things.

—**Cultivate your own personal growth** through classes you want to take or groups you want to join. Your life isn't over; your freedom has just begun. Jump in and you'll see that you'll soon adapt to this new season.

—**Institute game night!** We frequently had game night with our kids over the years and now we still play games. A blog I follow by Sheila Gregoire has a great post with a list of two-player board games: "To Love, Honor, and Vacuum: 20 Two Player Games to Play with Your Husband."[13]

Stay in Love

Lyrics and music by Debbie Cunningham

Oh, I wanna stay in love
Wanna stay in love with you
Wanna stay in love
Oh, I wanna stay in love
Wanna stay in love with you
That's why I said "I do"

All these little things that come in between us
If we let them they will tear us apart
We need to start fighting for, not with each other
Working to protect each other's hearts
Oh, I wanna stay in love
Wanna stay in love with you
Wanna stay in love

Oh, I wanna stay in love
Wanna stay in love with you
That's why I said "I do"

Angry words or quiet desperation
Wounded souls, drifting we will go
Unresolved we will find another reason
To build a wall where love used to grow

Oh, oh, oh I wanna stay in luh-uh-ove
I wanna stay in luh-uh-ove with you (oh, I'm not bailing)
Oh, oh, oh I wanna stay in luh-uh-ove
I wanna stay in luh-uh-ove with you

Oh, I wanna stay in love
Wanna stay in love with you
Wanna stay in love

Oh, I wanna stay in love
Wanna stay in love with you
That's why I said "I do"

CHAPTER TWELVE
Stopping the Drift

Real intimacy makes us feel alive like we've been found,
as if someone finally took the time to peer into the depths
of our soul and really see us there. Until then, until we
experience true intimacy, we will feel passed over and
ignored, like someone is looking right through us.

—*Shana Schutte*[14]

While I was writing these pages, I was also finishing the last writings of the songs on my album, *A Million Kisses*. I really wanted to write a song to communicate my intentions to work through issues of our relationship and, if necessary, fight to stay in love. Thus, the title "Stay in Love." Reminding my darling that I'm not going anywhere. He can't get rid of me that easily! Being intentional is hard at times. Life is flying by at a dizzying pace, and it's easy to just be bogged down with what everyone needs but you and your spouse. Especially in this middle season, you may have additional job pressure, aging parents to care for, college expenses, other financial obligations, and family events or commitments that overwhelm your schedule and your time. I encourage you to be mindful of it.

Many couples find themselves in a season of drifting apart in this season. It may be because of life circumstances that have affected their relationship, or it may be through neglect of one another. Either way, it is important to pay attention to it. Often, what begins as a drift grows into an emotional affair if left unattended. We were made for intimacy. We crave to be truly "known." That in and of itself is a God-given trait. There is nothing wrong with that but sometimes the way we go about it lends itself to a slippery slope. So, when we begin to drift in our relationship with our spouse, we will look elsewhere to fill that void of intimacy. Thus, temptation can enter the scene. With the birth of the Internet came amazing capabilities to connect us with information from anywhere. Social media sites then allowed us to connect with people around the globe as well. These are amazing tools that can be used for good or destruction. It is all in the hands of the user. However, it can be a danger zone for relationships. Now, more than ever before in our history, we have access to almost anyone we want via social media. People are connecting online to old boyfriends or girl-friends and picking up where they left off. I have heard so many stories of affairs starting just from a re-connect of an old love when their current relationship was lacking.

It is not that we cannot be friends or have a conversation with the opposite sex. However, we cannot be nonchalant about it either. We need to check ourselves and have accountability online. We need to safeguard our marriages with good bound-aries. Good boundaries start with not being secretive. We must not have conversations with someone that we wouldn't want our spouse to hear or see. Affairs used to take time to evolve, and now the Internet has made the seduction happen so quickly and so subtly. Just through an email or text, a relationship can go from friendship to emotional affair in hours if we cultivate it.

I'm concerned that we have become much too casual in our use of social media when it comes to protecting our marriage relationship, and it can very quickly widen the gap of the drifting apart we may feel. How do we know, then, if our friendships are crossing the line? In an article from *HuffPost*, Sheri Meyers says,

"If you're having intimate talks and sharing things you should only be sharing with your primary partner, or you're sending late night 'just thinking of you' flirty texts, you're not having just an innocent friendship."—Sheri Meyers[15]

Understand this can happen even if initially you were not looking for it. It happens to good men and women when they are struggling to find that emotional intimacy they so deeply crave with their spouse. Something is missing in the marriage relationship, which makes them vulnerable to temptation. If it seems that you and your spouse are drifting apart, say something. Don't ignore it, think it will go away, or treat it as harmless. You have to cultivate your relationship in these times so your spouse isn't looking elsewhere to find emotional intimacy.

Once emotional intimacy has been established with someone outside of your marriage, you are treading on thin ice. It doesn't matter that you didn't "intend" to get so closely intimate with someone. What matters is what is happening now in that friendship, your marriage, and the steps you are taking to change your course of action. Often, when someone is having an emotional affair, they become distant from their spouse and physical intimacy wanes as well. If this is happening, have an honest but compassionate conversation with your spouse.

Remember, Scripture teaches that any one of us can succumb to temptation given the right circumstances. Also, realize that your marriage is under siege. You need to see it as a wakeup call for your relationship. It has to be dealt with quickly, so it doesn't become a full-blown affair. Use of technology is not the only problem here with emotional attachment. Learning to set boundaries in everyday relationships with the opposite sex is important too. In this day and age, many affairs start in the workplace. Of course, we can work with the opposite sex without an issue, but we still must cultivate our time with our co-workers wisely. You can meet up in the breakroom and no one is the wiser. If you are finding unnecessary reasons to speak to a co-worker just because it feeds you emotionally, it is an issue. When light-hearted banter with a coworker or a working lunch becomes something you crave, it is time to put on the breaks and reassess your boundaries. I know several friends who will not meet or have lunch with the opposite sex alone. Even in a public place and even if they are truly just friends. It is a way they honor their spouse and put up a boundary to protect their relationship. I have male friends who I work with who won't send an email or text unless they copy their spouse. I'm okay with that. You have to decide what you both need in that boundary for both of you to feel comfortable. It is important to establish that together.

My husband works primarily with women and has for twenty-five years. He's a great guy, charming and fun, and people really like to be around him. I'm aware of that. For us, we set boundaries early in our marriage. At one point with his job, he was having lunch with co-workers a lot. Sometimes it was all women and my darling husband. That was fine. It was the team that he managed. However, sometimes it would end up being just him and one woman. That bothered me. I was at home raising a little one, feeling less than attractive while cooking, cleaning, changing diapers all day, and he was out to lunch with intelligent, well-dressed, lovely women. So, I mentioned it to him.

He said, "Well, I didn't plan to have lunch with just one woman. Everybody bailed, and I didn't know until I got to the restaurant. But from now on I will let you know when I'm going out and with whom, so you know. And you are always welcome to meet us if you like."

It was reaffirming to hear that he cared enough about our relationship to communicate with me about his lunch plans. From that day forward, he made it a practice to let me know when he was going out to lunch and with whom. He didn't have to. He hadn't broken my trust in any way, but he honored my discomfort with the situation. Over the years I have gone to many of those lunches. I got to know the people he worked with and that made all the difference for me. We did this, mind you, before there was even an inkling of a slippery slope.

We just saw these lunches as a potential hazard, so we put a plan in place. Mindful practices in our marriage are important.

However, that's when I realized how important it was for me to be mindful of what I was presenting to him when he came home too. Even though my stay-at-home mom working attire was less than stellar, I could still put make-up on and fix my hair before he came home and tidy up the house. In all honesty, that did not always happen! As much as I tried, there were days when the kids were sick and I was a mess when he came home, but I worked on it. I'm still mindful of it. Only now he works from home, too, so we both have to be mindful of it! Tempting to stay in your PJs all day when you work at home but not very appealing to your mate. To me this is just another part of safeguarding our marriage. Giving each other our best self instead of the bottom of the barrel.

We've always had a practice of calling each other when we are working out of town. At the very least, we have a daily text, but usually it is a phone call to stay connected. Even if it is just to say, "Long day. I'm exhausted. But I just wanted to call and say I love you." The intention and practice of connecting is there. That helps us when we are apart. We call each other if we change plans or have to come home late too. It is out of respect and a courtesy we extend to one another. It is just a practice that has served us in our relationship over the years and helped us not drift apart. These practices become habits in our relationship. What is helpful is that good habits kick in even when our relationship has been strained by a disagreement. I mean, we are human, and we certainly get frustrated with each other.

We also have a practice of date nights. I will say that Kenneth and Lisa, and a few other friends we have, do a much better job at the consistency of date nights in their marriage than we do. We try to go do something fun weekly. It's just not every Friday. We learned early in our marriage that we had to keep dating. In fact, when we first got married, we stopped going on dates. After all, we had 24/7 access to each other now. Why would we "plan" a date to see each other? We quickly realized we needed time set aside to have fun together. We both were working crazy schedules, and we were not actually seeing each other as much as we thought we would. Sometimes we literally passed each other in the hallway of our apartment. He was coming home, and I was going to work. We didn't even have children at the time, but we both were overscheduled with our jobs and volunteer work. Good pursuits but just not in balance. So, we began to say *no* to many things. That took some courage to disappoint people. But for us, it protected our marriage by cultivating time together. Sometimes we just ordered a pizza and stayed home and watched Friday night TV, but we carved out that time to be together and that is what matters.

"Untended fires soon die and become just a pile of ashes."—Anonymous

It seems in our society today that we are constantly over-scheduled. It is hard to get a serious discussion in if we are always running from here to there. If you have children, it doubles or triples the amount of downtime you already don't have. We have to be intentional about spending time as a couple; if we don't, our relationship will fizzle away. Otherwise, one day we will be scratching our heads wondering what happened to our relationship and who the stranger is sleeping in our bed.

Practices for Staying in Love and Stopping the Drift:

—**Honest communication.** If you realize you and your spouse are drifting, you need to say something. Awareness is the first step. Perhaps you and your spouse can find ways to connect once a week if the roommate dilemma has appeared.

—**Have boundaries in your relationship with the opposite sex.** If you realize you are cultivating *emotional intimacy* with someone other than your spouse, you need to stop now. Call a trusted friend or seek out counseling. THIS IS IMPORTANT. Take steps to protect your relationship. Communicate. Go to marriage counseling. A licensed counselor can advise the two of you to set boundaries for your relationship and show you how to untangle yourself from an unhealthy emotional attachment.

—**Carve out time together.** Start dating your spouse again. Check out date night ideas on Pinterest or search date night ideas online. Making it a priority is really important. Go away for a weekend if you can to reconnect.

—**FUN.** Find something fun you both enjoy and go do that. Even if it is just dinner with friends or trying a new restaurant. I've mentioned this many times, but it is really important to find fun in your relationship again. Play cards or go to the game section at your local store and find one to try.

CHAPTER THIRTEEN
Diffusing Temptation

No temptation has overtaken you except what is common to mankind. And God is faithful; He will not let you be tempted beyond what you can bear. But when you are tempted, he will also provide a way out so that you can endure it.

—*1 Corinthians 10:13*

FLEE from sexual immorality. All other sins a person commits are outside the body, but whoever sins sexually, sins against their own body.

—*1 Corinthians 6:18*

When I picked up the phone, I heard her shaking voice on the other end. She barely said my name before she broke into sobbing cries. "What's wrong?" I asked. "I found texts on his phone to another woman. My heart hurts. I feel so broken. I can't believe he's had an affair. I don't want to die but right now I don't want to live either. I want the pain to stop."

My heart sank. Another friend's marriage was crumbling after forty years. Forty. When I hung up the phone, I wept for my friends. I know them well, and I love them both. They are good people, and they are strong Christians. They love God and seek to follow Him and serve Him. They have grown children and grandchildren. They have been through harsh difficulties over the years, and I've watched them fall at God's feet in gut-wrenching circumstances and seek His face. I prayed for them. My heart now ached that another friend was seduced by the voice of the enemy. Because of that, two more marriages were now about to fall apart.

Be alert and of sober mind. Your enemy the devil prowls around like a roaring lion looking for someone to devour. Resist him, standing firm in the faith, because you know that the family of believers throughout the world is undergoing the same kind of sufferings. **(1 Peter 5:8–9)**

Temptation is not a respecter of persons. It doesn't matter if you are young or old, married or single, Christian or not. None of us are exempt from temptation. My fear, though, is that we are not taking this matter seriously.

When the warning signs begin to show up in our rela-tionships and we are tempted, what do we do? Do we apply God's Word to the matter and flee? Or do we entertain the thoughts and feelings associated with it and, thus, *invite* temptation in to sit at the table of our heart, while we decide what to do?

There should be no hesitation. Easier said than done, I know, but we should run away from the danger. That is what the Scrip-ture states. Why are we playing around and cultivating it? It isn't easy because we are always tempted with something we like. We like the taste of the food or the drink, but we have too much. We like the way we feel with a certain person, and we don't want to say *no* to that. Many of us have been there in one situation or another. The only thing that is going to keep us on the high road when tempted is applying God's Word. That's the only way.

HE will provide a way of escape. He says so in His Word, but are we looking for it? Are we doing what he already told us to do? When we are standing next to a woman or man who is not our spouse and we feel a sudden rush of attraction, do we take a step back? It might be our co-worker or boss. It might be someone who is on the same volunteer team at church. It might be our neighbor. What do we do? Now, I am asking you, have you thought about what you would do? When we live our lives in wishy-washy indecision, nothing gets accomplished. It is scientifically proven that we accomplish what we decide in advance to do. We choose our path by either making conscious decisions or not. Either way, we choose.

It is not a sin to be tempted. I feel like this needs to be repeated. Temptation itself is not the sin. What you do with it becomes the sin. I have heard spouses say after an affair, "I just don't know how this happened." Well, someone listened to the voice of the enemy and followed it. That is what happened. I have been mulling this over a lot. I have even asked God many times, "Why is this happening?" He reminded me to go back to Genesis. To see that even in the Garden of Eden, where Adam and Eve were living in a perfect environment and walking with God face to face, mind you, that they were tempted. Someone listened to the whisper of the enemy. It was very subtle. The devil didn't say, "Go, eat the fruit of that tree in the center of the garden." He simply asked a suggestive question. Let's look at it.

Genesis 3:1–5

1. *Now the serpent was more crafty than any of the wild animals the Lord God had made. He said to the woman, "Did God really say, 'You must not eat from any tree in the garden'?"*

2. *The woman said to the serpent, "We may eat fruit from the trees in the garden,*

3. *but God did say, 'You must not eat fruit from the tree that is in the middle of the garden, and you must not touch it, or you will die.'"*

4. *"You will certainly not die," the serpent said to the woman.*

5. *"For God knows that when you eat from it your eyes will be opened, and you will be like God, knowing good and evil."*

What is the enemy whispering to us in sexual temptation? He whispers things like, "Is it really a sin if you are only talking? This is okay. It is just a conversation and after all, this is your co-worker. You are just working, not dating."

And we subtly agree. We say *yes* to "this is just talking." But it digresses from there because we have not turned away immediately. We have not politely ended our conversation, excused ourselves, and gotten away from it. We have entertained it. The next day, when we see that person, the attraction feels stronger. Feelings are neither right nor wrong. They are just feelings. You can't control how you feel, but you can control how you respond to those feelings.

First of all, we need to pray. We should probably call a trusted friend right away and have them pray with us because then we have immediate accountability.

Accountability is a safeguard. Secrets kill us.

Trying to do this independently destroys us. I know this may sound drastic, but I am telling you, I have heard it over and over again from people who have had affairs how quickly the impulses strengthen for the relationship outside of their marriage because someone didn't turn away at the first impulse. The first feelings in a relationship are like hot sparks in a fire.

Every choice we make to ignore the sparks flying (thinking we won't get burned) is careless. We have to put the fire out right away. Remember, the enemy is not playing around. He is seeking to devour and destroy. We need to not play around or make excuses either. We need to see it as it is. This is *warfare* to destroy our marriage. Even as I write these words, my heart wants to scream, "Mayday, mayday, we are in trouble here. Send help!" Because it is a little like that, but we don't want to admit it. Even Jesus said to the disciples, "Watch and pray that you don't fall into temptation. The spirit is willing, but the flesh is weak." It isn't weak to ask for help. It is wise.

I have heard people share, too, that they didn't tell their spouse when they first felt the attraction because they were afraid to upset their spouse. I understand that, but an affair is going to destroy your spouse, and your marriage is going to be over. It isn't that God cannot resurrect it. He can. I've seen that many times too. The marriage relationship will die first though. And you will be starting over in a new normal for your relationship. Wouldn't it be better then, if we viewed temptation as the warning sign that it is and do something about it the moment it shows up?

One of my friends did that. She had been feeling ignored by her husband. He was really busy with his work, and she noticed she was starting to have feelings for a co-worker. This was not her intention, but it continued to grow stronger. Finally, she went home and told her husband. She realized that to protect her marriage she needed to ask for what she needed and be honest about how feeling neglected was cultivating this attraction.

In her heart, she had no desire to have an affair, and yet she felt tempted. As soon as she told her husband, the feelings for the other man went away. Now it wasn't a secret anymore. She brought it to the light of day by telling her spouse. She and her husband realized they needed to spend more time together and not let their hearts slip into cruise control. Basically, the temptation for another man was just a symptom of the unhealthy state of their marriage. Is it possible for us to start seeing temptation this way? As a wake-up call? Maybe we need to communicate this a little better at churches too. Some people are walking around ashamed to share struggles even at church for fear of judgment. Yet, we profess that Jesus died to forgive us of our sins. We are sinners. Every single one of us.

For ALL have sinned and fallen short of the glory of God. (Romans 3:23)

When we keep these struggles in secret and are not seeking to bring them under the counsel of the Word of God, we will fall. We need to have a safe place to do that and find accountability.

It is our isolation and silence that will get us into trouble. If no one knows what we are struggling with, it is easy to step into the flame. We are like moths drawn to the flicker of the light at times. Too often we wait to ask God for help *after* we have already stepped over the line instead of *before*. He is more than willing to help us, but once we have stepped over the line, it is much more complicated and difficult for us, for then it is like quicksand. A friend who had an affair shared later that she repeatedly asked God to get her out of it, but she didn't walk away from the relationship. She knew it was wrong, and the man she had an affair with did too. When you are with someone other than your spouse and you hear yourself say out loud or under your breath, "This is wrong; we need to stop," then you need to make a run for it. It was only when she was caught that the answer to that prayer came to fruition. Did God expose her to answer that prayer? Maybe, but the damage was already done. Her family fell apart, and the marriage ended. I don't know why she didn't come to her husband or friends for help when it started. She secretly cultivated an affair instead. Her husband is not without his faults and their marriage was having troubles, but it doesn't excuse her choice for breaking her marriage vow. We are all responsible in our marriage struggles, but the one who breaks the vow is responsible for the affair.

We are all responsible for our choices.

But it takes two people to break a marriage vow. The other person responsible in this case is the man who also had this affair with her. He could have stopped it, but he chose not to. I've watched too many friends throw away their marriages (and destroy their family) for a fleeting moment. It's heart-wrenching. These two were both professing Christians. Please hear me. I am not saying it is easy to turn from temptation. Only with God's help can we do that. The flesh is weak. The struggle is real. In order to keep us from walking down this path, we must know the Word of God and apply it to the temptation. It's the only offensive weapon we have in this.

The WORD of God is our sword to fight when we are in a battle. We must take every thought captive and do what the Scripture says when the whispers of the enemy come our way to seduce us from God's best.

Temptation is a serious matter. We need to get it to the light of day if we are going to get out from under it. It is the enemy of our souls that is entangling us in its snare, but we also have responsibility to resist what we know is wrong. Resist the devil and he will flee from you. It's interesting to me that temptation starts and ends with fleeing. Scripture says that we must flee temptation. And when we resist the temptation (by fleeing it), the enemy will flee away from us. Stand firm my friend.

Practices for Resisting Temptation:

—**Use your sword to fight.** The Word of God is our sword. Read it and do what it says to do. God has given us instructions for living and for fighting when temptation strikes.

—**Flee sexual temptation.** Get serious and go the opposite direction, the opposite side of the room.

—**Seek out accountability.** You need to have someone to be accountable to in this. Keeping temptation a secret will just fuel your desire. Interestingly, if you speak it out loud to your spouse or a trusted friend, it loses ground because someone else knows. They can pray for you, too, and check in with you to see how you are doing.

—**Communicate.** Temptation frequently is a wake-up call to something not right in your relationship. Pray and talk about it.

—**Get marriage counseling.** If you are struggling in your marriage relationship, please seek out counseling before you give in to temptation.

—**Ask Jesus and the Holy Spirit for wisdom.** From Pastor Mike Smith, Christ Community Church on Genesis 3:1–5: "Regarding Satan's temptation of Eve (and Adam). Satan saw the weakness in their plan to follow God's one law (one law!!) by placing a fence around that law ("you must not touch it"). This was not part of what God told Adam (2:17). Satan saw the weakness in their plan to obey God. They were trying to do it in their own strength! At any point, Eve (or Adam) could have asked God if what Satan (through the serpent) was saying was true. When tempted, not only look to Scripture, but ask Jesus and the Holy Spirit to be with you and help you as you make choices!"

Anniversary Song

Lyrics and music by Debbie Cunningham

Happy Anniversary
Celebrate the memory
Of the moment
When one love was made for two

Happy Anniversary
Reminisce tenderly
Be present in each day
Is my wish for you

May you remember
All the love that said, "I do"
As I sing
Happy Anniversary to you

(Tag)
May you remember
All the love that said, "I do"
As I sing
Happy Anniversary
May you two forever be
Happy Anniversary...... to you

CHAPTER FOURTEEN

Celebration and Gratitude

We all have life storms, and when we get the rough times
and we recover from them, we should celebrate that we
got through it. No matter how bad it may seem, there's
always something beautiful you can find.

—*Mattie Stepanek, American poet*[16]

My in-laws were truly a delightful couple. They were married over fifty years before they passed. In the early years, they were sharecroppers. They worked long days in the field and when six children came into the picture, long days at home. They lived through the Great Depression, and they learned to value what they had even if it was meager. They appreciated the simplest things together: a beautiful sunset, a walk together by the ocean shore, or the first rose on the bush. In fact, they had a competition each year to see who saw the first rosebud in bloom in their yard and when they did, they cut it off and presented it to the other as a token of love. It was sweet and lighthearted fun. At the end of the day, it was just another way to say *I love you*. Now, they had their moments of disagreement and hard seasons too. However, they chose to honor one another, pray for each other, and love unconditionally. They danced, too, whenever they had the chance. It was fun and celebratory. I always loved watching them dance. They delighted in one another.

My parents are another couple whose marriage relationship I admire. As I shared earlier, the man I call Dad is actually my stepdad. When he met my mom, I'm sure he never envisioned being the father to four children who weren't biologically his. He actually never anticipated having children at all. The day before my wedding, he told me that even though it wasn't in his original plan for his life, he was so thankful that God didn't let him miss the blessing of having kids. When he married my mom three years after they met, he adopted all four of us so we could be a family united in name as well. The point is this… there were more than a few people who wondered if that relationship would last. I love watching my parents together. I can only imagine how hard it was in a new marriage as my stepdad moved into the role of husband and father of four kids simultaneously.

Of course, there were stressful times as in all blended families. But when they said, "I do" their intent was forever. They committed to each other and to being a family. Their faith is very much a part of their story, and they loved each other through the storms of having four teenagers at once! What I love now is that they are enjoying their empty nest time, spending the couple time together they didn't get initially. They are both retired and getting to travel and enjoy grandkids. They spend a lot of time helping others too. They have moved countless people across the country. They care for widows and the elderly in their proximity as well as family members. They just have serving hearts, and when they see a need, they lovingly serve people—*together*. It is a connecting point for them. They have a beautiful love story, and they value each other. I am so thankful to be a part of their life as a daughter. They, too, will tell you that faith, commitment, and gratitude for little things plays a huge part in their relationship.

It was with my parents and my in-laws in mind that I originally wrote "Anniversary Song." I also wanted a song to sing to couples who attend my concerts when celebrating their anniversary. I *love* to sing to couples and celebrate with them! I believe in celebrating little milestones, not just big ones. I always have. We even have a glass in our cabinet that has the words "celebrate, congrats, woohoo" on it. If you come to my house and you just got a promotion or an A on that final exam, or if it is your birthday you will be drinking out of it! It's just a small way that I can say, "Congrats! We share your excitement!"

Gratitude and celebrating what we have are a big part of happiness.

Sometimes we forget to celebrate. Remembering and celebrating are important! As far as anniversaries go, remembering why you fell in love in the first place is a great reflection. Those first moments in a relationship are golden. Life is short. Celebrate the little things.

We never know how much time we have, and we need to value what we do have, while we have it. It is easy to lose focus on the preciousness of today… the mundane of going to work, cooking, cleaning, or climbing the corporate ladder can do that to you. When tragedy hits we value what we have, realizing it can be taken at any moment. Sadly, I have heard of a few young widows who wish they had been more present and celebrated their relationship. Don't wait for that.

Be intentional in savoring the moments. I really believe many couples miss out on this. It's really important to set aside time to celebrate all that you are and have come through. Women are probably more attune to this. It is meaningful to us. I know that some feel the need to refuse to participate if they feel it's expected… like Valentine's Day for instance. (And I know holidays have become commercial rackets!) For most women I know, they just want to be remembered or thought of. And yes, a card or a flower is an action that says *I love you and I'm thinking of you*. It doesn't have to be expensive. Whatever "it" is, its value lies in the fact that you took the time and made your spouse a priority. Sometimes we feel ignored by one another. This goes both ways for husbands and wives for different reasons.

Taking the time to celebrate your relationship for your anniversary or celebrate your spouse on a birthday or Valentine's Day is like saying, "You are important to me and I want to remind you by celebrating this day." It is a gift to your spouse.

Some couples really struggle with this in their marriage relationship. One spouse wants to celebrate things and the other spouse refuses or doesn't want to feel obligated just because it is a holiday or an anniversary. I get that no one wants to be forced to buy a gift or do something if it is an expected thing. Here's the important caveat:

What if this celebrating and remembering your spouse is really a part of your spouse's love language? In other words, the way they *feel* loved by you? If you refuse, then are you really seeking to love them well?

You may have true feelings of love for your spouse, but if you don't communicate it to them in a way they understand, you are not truly communicating. Sometimes we fail at recognizing how our spouse feels love. You may do something you think is special and your spouse may not receive it as love at all. Gary Chapman wrote a wonderful book, *The 5 Love Languages*, to get you in touch with how you might be speaking a different love language than your spouse. Do you know what makes him or her feel loved? The book speaks of five ways people feel love:

1. Physical Touch
2. Acts of Service
3. Quality Time
4. Words of Affirmation
5. Receiving Gifts

Have you ever done something for your spouse to show them love and they didn't appreciate it? It's probably because you are loving them with *your love language* and *not theirs*. If you are trying to celebrate your spouse, make sure you are doing something that speaks love to them in the way they need to hear it. It's always good to be speaking the same language!

Although these are broad generalizations, sometimes a husband doesn't realize that although his wife appreciates him paying the bills and mowing the lawn, that doesn't speak love to her like a card on Valentine's Day or an unexpected flower or small gift that says *I'm thinking of you*. At the same time, men frequently feel love through physical touch or words of affirmation. Wives need to look at how they are speaking or not speaking love to their husbands through physical intimacy.

I will say this, a wife who feels well-loved outside of the bedroom has an easier time responding to her husband in the bedroom. Overall, both spouses need to be attentive to the *love language* of the other if we are going to choose to love each other well.

The world will distract us with a million things. If it's not your work, it is the kids, extended family, illness, unfulfilled hopes, or financial trouble. All of these things can rob you of joy in your marriage. It's good practice to reflect on the good you have shared with one another over the years and celebrate it.

When our kids were young, we once went to an unusual marriage conference. We were feeling a little flat in our relationship and knew we needed to connect. It wasn't so much about celebrating but being in gratitude for what we had and tending to it. What we loved about this conference was that it was more about experiencing adventure together than someone lecturing us on marriage. (Okay, I'm not a big adventure seeker, but life felt stale and I was game to try something new and he was happy to not sit around and talk about his feelings. Win/Win.) I was afraid we wouldn't have much to talk about except the kids. We had to pick three adventures to engage in over the weekend, and we had free time for a date night on Saturday evening. I don't remember our options, but our adventure choices were hiking, mountain biking, and outdoor rock climbing and repelling. Hiking was fine. Getting into the outdoors, appreciating nature. All good. About the mountain biking... did I mention we were not regular cyclists nor were we exactly in shape? Our mountain biking consisted of us finally pushing our bikes up the steep hills, laughing at how ridiculous we must look to all those ACTUALLY RIDING their bikes up the hill, and a delightful coast on the way down! It was fun regardless. Laughter is GOOD for the soul and learning to laugh at yourself is also good for your marriage.

Our last adventure was the most terrifying: climbing and repelling. Neither of us had done that before. They took us to a side of a mountain in Asheville, North Carolina, and our guides began setting up ropes and other equipment while we put on our thin rubber shoes and gear. Of course, they had each of us connected with ropes and a harness to a belayer below. The belayer's job was to anchor the rope and keep you steady as you climbed and when you descended. He also gave us instructions and encouragement when we experienced fear or difficulty in the climb. When they say you grip for dear life, they are not kidding! With each level, I scanned for a cranny in the rock to dig my toes into and the tiniest ledge for my fingers to grip while simultaneously breathing another prayer for courage. Even though this was recreational, this was the side of a cliff, not a manmade indoor climb center! I was certain that I would never reach the top but with my husband's encouragement and the belayer's instruction from below, I did.

Once there, I was ready to come down immediately. However, at my belayer's request, I turned my head around to see not only the view but also what I had accomplished before I made my descent. Some were afraid to look over the valley below but I'm so glad I did. It was exhilarating! I spent a few seconds truly breathing in that moment. It was spring, and the colors of flowers and trees down over the valley were stunning. I was gazing over not just where our climbing journey had begun but all the way to the deep valley below. My husband did the same and neither of us will ever forget it. We worked through something that was very challenging to us, and we accomplished it together. We came back from that weekend truly refreshed and refueled in our relationship. As I reflected on that, I realized a few things. Gazing on that valley made me think about marriage.

In marriage, when we scale new heights, we are starting out on a ledge together somewhere in the middle of a mountain, but each of us has made a journey separately to get to that ledge.

When we reach new heights together, it is a celebration of the entire journey, not just where the two of us began. Focusing and gripping for dear life to the mountain we are climbing is necessary at times but pausing to breathe and enjoy how far we have come is also a beautiful part of the journey. Just think what I would have missed if I hadn't taken the time to pause and look at the view before I came down from that triumph. We have a lot to be thankful for. Sometimes, it just takes a different perspective to see it. (By the way, we had a lot more to laugh about and talk about at dinner that night too!) Taking this time away together is a form of celebrating and cultivating the good in our relationship.

My husband and I do love to celebrate life. We especially love to celebrate birthdays and to make the birthday person feel special and valued. It is very hard for us to surprise each other but for our fiftieth birthdays we both were working very hard to do just that. I remember thinking about my husband and how he loved to not just sit around at a party but to do an activity of some kind. He also had expressed a few months prior that he had been missing his friendships of younger years and that he really wanted to connect with his old softball buddies.

So, for his birthday I contacted several of them to see if they would meet him for coffee at a local shop and then began plotting how to get him there. He was helping to build a set for our son's musical performance that Saturday, but I made arrangements for him to leave by 2:10 p.m. I asked him to call me when he left because I had some birthday instructions for him. When he got to the car, I had left a poem in his glove compartment stating that he was to go to the shop. My friend was meeting him with a fresh shirt and he was to order coffee and sit down. Three friends of life past would visit him: one at 3 p.m., at 4 p.m. and at 5 p.m. His birthday is January 4, so *A Christmas Carol* was fresh on my mind. (I had this in a rhyme, but I cannot even remember it now!) The men came one after another and they spent an hour of conversation and laughter with him. My husband was delighted, and his friends said it was a gift to them too. Men don't often take the time to get together and reconnect with their guy friends like we women do, but they appreciate it when it happens.

Then, when he returned home, I had a big surprise party waiting. It was a mystery murder party. There was a 1920's theme, complete with costumed friends and gangster plot. It was so much fun! I had a costume all ready for him when he got home. Poor guy! He was quite exhausted from three hours of talking and then a house full of friends at the party. It was really memorable for both of us.

A few years later, when I turned fifty, Derek was looking to surprise me with a special gift. He knows I love the beach, so he threw me a Hawaii Five-0 party, which was lovely, with a few of our neighbors and friends. But he did something really special that will forever be my most favorite gift. Fifty days before I turned fifty, a friend called to wish me a happy birthday and tell me what she appreciated about our friendship. I thought that was sweet of her. Then the next day another friend called to do the same, and I realized that Derek had set a plan in motion. A friend or family member called each day for the fifty days leading up to my fiftieth birthday. It really was the best gift I have ever had. Know why? Because it totally made me feel loved. I feel love when I connect and have quality time or conversation with people I care about. He reached out to friends I hadn't talked to in years. Even a few special teachers I had in elementary and high school. It was the best gift ever! And it didn't cost him a dime... just time and thoughtfulness.

Celebrate life. It's your life. New job? Celebrate it! Married ten, twenty, thirty, forty years? Celebrate it with a special dinner, a night out, or even a weekend away. There is no guarantee that we will have another minute, let alone another day or year. Be present every day. First day of spring? Bake cookies or take a romantic walk and be thankful. Celebrate what you have this moment while you work toward something new in the future.

Celebrating is just a really a fun way to express gratitude for what you have to be thankful for right now.

It creates joy, and joyful people are happier and have better relationships. My Grammy frequently said to me as a child, "There is always something to be thankful for, you just have to look for the silver lining sometimes." I say, "Sometimes, we have to create the silver lining."

Practices for Staying in Love through Gratitude and Celebration:

—**Pray. Give thanks to God for what you do have.** We've talked a lot about asking God for what we need, but it is also important to thank Him for what He has already given us.

—**Practice being grateful in your relationship.** He might forget your birthday, but he works hard and provides for your family. She might not be the perfect housekeeper, but she loves you unconditionally. Focus on that for now and pray that God will make your spouse sensitive to how you feel love.

—**Celebrate little things now.** Don't wait for someday. Celebrate an accomplishment or a milestone in your life. Make a special dinner or toast an accomplishment with champagne and dessert. Use the special china or the beautiful lingerie. Take a weekend or one night to get away and be present with one another. OR save money and take the BIG trip you always dreamed of, but don't wait so long that it never comes to pass. Little milestones are worth celebrating! Celebration breeds joy, and joyful people have better relationships.

—**Celebrate someone else.** Surprise someone. Bake cookies or a cake together and take it to your neighbor. You'll be surprised by the joy you feel.

—**Read *The 5 Love Languages* by Gary Chapman** and see if you can better speak your spouse's love language. It is a great way to build more meaningful connection in your marriage.

There is a quiz online to get you started:

http://www.5lovelanguages.com/profile/couples/

Chocolate

Lyrics and music by Debbie Cunningham[17]

They say that diamonds are a girl's best friend
But I don't see no diamonds bringing me comfort at a long
   day's end
When I'm tired and feeling stressed
And I climb those stairs to decompress
I've got something that'll make my heart sing
That will rival any diamond ring

I've got Chocolate
Gotta have that chocolate
Chocolate is a girl's best friend
It is the food for any kind of mood
Chocolate is a girl's best friend

Ask any man you know
There are days when his lady is oh, so low
When she's sad and feeling blue
And it seems there's nothing he can do
I've got something that will make her heart sing
That will rival any of that bling!

Give her Chocolate
Gotta have that chocolate
Chocolate is a girl's best friend
It is the food for any kind of mood
Chocolate is a girl's best friend

(Bridge)
Oh, we've got hot chocolate sweet and steamy
Milk chocolate smooth and dreamy
Dark chocolate, bittersweet
Never met chocolate that a woman couldn't eat

(Tag)
It doesn't give flack, no, it doesn't talk back,
Chocolate is a girl's best friend
It never teases but it sure appeases
Chocolate is a girl's best friend, chocolate is a girl's best friend,
Chocolate is a girl's best friend

CHAPTER FIFTEEN
Chocolate and Dance Lessons

My momma always said life is like a box of chocolates.
You never know what you're gonna get.

—*Forrest Gump*[18]

I wanted to introduce you to another dear friend as we finish our little journey together. My friend Anita and I share a love of seeing the glass half full, laughter, and chocolate! She lives her life purposing to bring smiles to those around her, and I truly love that about her. Of course, one of the reasons I wrote "Chocolate" was because I wanted to make women smile.

Around the world there is an association of romance and indulgence to chocolate. Why else would it be such a big seller on Valentine's Day? Chocolate companies use words like *savor, melt, bliss,* and *it's your moment, so live each day to the fullest* to lure us in to the pleasures of chocolate in their advertising. I mean, most women *do* relate to a love of chocolate and a few guys too, so I've been told. It can't solve all your problems, but it can make life a little sweeter.

Adding a little sweetness to your life or a funny song about chocolate for that matter makes life a little more enjoyable. Those words are good words for your relationship too; savor it, melt, find bliss, and it's your moment, so live each day to the fullest with your spouse! Who doesn't want that? Forrest Gump was right about life though. Life is like a box of chocolates. You never know what you're going to get until you open the box. However, what do you do when you don't like the flavor?

There will always be flavors in our life and marriage experiences that are less than your favorite. It's what you do with it that will make or break your relationships. My friend Anita is a master at this, and I've learned from her over the years. We became friends unexpectedly when her great-nephew, Parker, was diagnosed with leukemia. He was three years old. In an effort to help her great nephew's family, Anita's son, Tracey, created a "flat Parker" (inspired by the book, *Flat Stanley*) and sent him around the United States to travel for the real Parker while he was going through three years of cancer treatments. People all across the country volunteered to receive "flat Parker" and take pictures with him in their local area; they then sent those pictures back to Tracey, who compiled them and posted them on a Facebook page for the real Parker and his family to see. Tracey created something fun and positive for Parker's family to focus on through those difficult years. They also shared the journey publicly and ended up raising money for cancer research in the process. (Parker is cancer-free now, by the way. If you want to know more about their story and the Flat Parker Project, check the Notes at the end of this book.)[19]

We were one of the families that volunteered. That is how I met Anita because she was involved with her son on the whole project. During the time we had "Flat Parker" I happened to be in the studio recording "Chocolate" and a few other songs for my album, *A Million Kisses*. So, we sent photos of Flat Parker in the recording studio. Perfect for a Nashville tour!

Anita is one of the most positive people I have ever met. You would never know, however, that on occasion her own life has looked a little like an episode of *I Love Lucy*. But we love Lucille Ball and all her crazy antics. Even if it didn't turn out the way Lucy planned, *she always made the best of it*. Anita has that attitude in real life. I mentioned in an earlier chapter that she and her husband, Alex, ride their tractor around their farm and watch fireflies in the evening. They've been married fifty-two years. But I must tell you of an occasion when Alex *could* have been in deep trouble with Anita.

Alex and Anita live on a 200-acre farm in Missouri. At one time they had over 250 sheep, cattle, and horses. When they first purchased the property, it had a log cabin house right in the middle of the land. The previous owners of the home had made two additions to the cabin by attaching a train boxcar on one end for living space, and they had made a wooden, lean-to type structure on the other end of the house. The "lean-to" roof literally sloped from the peak of the cabin down to a six-foot wall. This lower end housed the kitchen of the home and the bathroom. In fact, the ceiling was so low in the kitchen they were always breaking light bulbs. The previous owners were less than five feet tall, and Anita and Alex are five feet, nine inches and six feet, respectively! Even the kitchen counters were lower than the traditional height. It was quite frustrating for them. They talked about the possibility of renovating someday.

They needed to do some work on the property that required a backhoe, so they called a company to send one out. They lived in such a rural area that it took six months to get one out there!

The day finally arrived, and the backhoe operator showed up. Anita had taken her daughter Gigi out to riding lessons after school. On a whim, and knowing that it could be six more months until he could get that kind of equipment back on the farm, Alex decided while he had the backhoe onsite that perhaps it was time to start the kitchen remodel.

So, he asked the guy, "Hey, if I cut those beams in the ceiling of the kitchen and bathroom, can you use your backhoe to knock down that side of the house?"

Backhoe operator "Umm… Did you *ask* your wife?"

Alex, "No, but it'll be fine."

Backhoe operator, "Do you want to *stay* married?"

Alex, "She'll be fine with it."

Imagine Anita's surprise when she came home that afternoon in May to find a gaping hole in the side of her house… and no usable kitchen or bathroom?

I asked her, "How in the world did you respond to that?" (I think I might have killed my husband!) She laughed and said, "Well, I knew he must have a plan. He always has a vision. So, I got excited that I was finally going to get a new kitchen!" Alex put up tarps to keep any rain out, and they worked on a remodel from May until October. She said, "It was summer, so we made use of the old outhouse that happened to still be on the property, the creek that runs through our land, and we bought a huge stock tub for bathing. We filled twenty-gallon jugs with water and let them sit in the sun all day to get warm. Then we bathed under the stars at night. It was completely private, and the kids thought it was fun. We cooked on a hot plate and used a Crock Pot." Alex said, "I have the most loving, patient wife a man could ever have. Believe me, I've done more than just that one thing. She always trusts me, and we just make the best of the process. We both enjoy the creative process of building and remodeling. Enjoying the process together is one of the best parts of our journey."

I love that Anita "trusted he had a plan" and that she was flexible with living in the not-perfect housing situation. She also said, "There was no point in getting mad. Life is too short. It's not as if I could change anything. That side of the house was gone! We just had to move forward with the remodel."

What a wise woman. Laughable though it may be, that event has not only become a fond memory but a connecting point for them. I'm certain there were times it was frustrating. I'm certain that by September, when school started again, it was less than convenient. But they kept moving forward, *together*. Anita and Alex know firsthand that another day is not guaranteed. Two years into their marriage, Alex got a very serious infection in his back that landed him in the hospital for back surgery. There were only two other cases with this same infection in their area and both were due to cancer. However, when they operated on Alex it was not cancer, for which they are eternally grateful. They have lived appreciating every day they have together from that moment on.

I truly wonder what would happen in our marriages if we began to really believe that *nothing will be impossible with God.* (Luke 1:37 ESV) If we lived in light of the *truth of the gospel* that *his* love can transform our marriages, as we trust him and believe his Word. Jesus paid the price for all of our sins when He died on the cross, *not just to forgive us but also to restore us,* our relationships, and to grant us a new life in Him. Wherever you are in your marriage journey, I am praying that God will give you faith to believe that He can transform your marriage as you seek Him in your relationship. Even if it is hard for you to believe, remember, God works through imperfect faith! So, step out in faith to trust Him, ask Him to lead you, and just see what happens!

May the Lord make your love increase and overflow for each other. **(1 Thessalonians 3:12a)**

Remember my friend David? I have one last detail to tell you about him. When they were first married, Tricia wanted David to take ballroom dancing lessons with her. He kept putting it off. Life was busy as he was building his career and there was plenty of time, or so he thought. She kept asking, and he kept procrastinating. When Tricia was unexpectedly diagnosed with multiple sclerosis, their world changed and suddenly she had to go into a wheelchair. Then they were out of time. David doesn't have a lot of regrets in his marriage, but he does regret waiting to dance.

A million kisses kind of love—*the kind that dances in the kitchen when the skies are turning gray. The one that holds you oh, so tight when the blues just won't go away.* I want that, don't you? Watching fireflies, playing games for date night, watching the sunset, presenting the first rose of the bush, or putting on music and spontaneously *dancing in the kitchen*. It's all about *connecting* to your spouse and cultivating the kind of love that lasts a lifetime.

Marriage is really what you make of it. So, take the class. Learn the steps. *Don't wait* to rekindle your romance and connection with one another because life is too short for that.

It really is true, you know. **Marriage *is* like dancing.**

It just takes a lot of practice to get better at all aspects of your relationship. You'll step on each other's toes, guaranteed. But try to laugh more than you get frustrated, and don't give up!

Remember, it's supposed to be to fun! Enjoy it and before you know it, you'll be dancing… at least across the kitchen floor.

Conclusion

For those of you who are really struggling in your marriage and wondering what to do next, I don't want to leave you without a plan, so I have a few suggestions.

1. Seek out counseling in your area. If your spouse doesn't want to go, then go for yourself. You can't change your spouse, but you can change your responses to what is happening in your relationship.

2. Contact a trusted pastor for advisement.

3. If you are in an abusive relationship, please call the national domestic abuse hotline: 1-800-799-7233. They will help you 24 hours a day, 7 days a week.

4. Review the additional resources listed here that I have found helpful over the years in my own life. Perhaps these would be beneficial to you as well.

5. Visit my website *www.debbiecunningham.net* for:

   • New/updated relationship resources.

   • FREE song downloads of "A Million Kisses" and "Chocolate."

- Links to other marriage websites and blogs that may be helpful.

Additional book resources you may find helpful:

- *The 5 Love Languages* by Gary Chapman
- *Laugh Your Way to a Better Marriage* by Mark Gungor
- *Love and Respect* by Dr. Emerson Eggerichs
- *Listen, Learn, Love* by Susie Albert Miller
- *The Marriage Ark* by Margaret Phillips
- *The DNA of Relationships* by Gary Smalley
- *Barbara and Susan's Guide to the Empty Nest* by Barbara Rainey and Susan Yates
- *After the Miracle* by David B. Hampton (addiction recovery/relationship resource)
- *The 7 Rings of Marriage* by Jackie Bledsoe

About the Author

Debbie Cunningham is a recording artist, author, and speaker. She graduated from Temple University with a Bachelor of Music in Voice Performance and has spent more than a decade in the music business as a songwriter and entertainer. She has recorded two albums; the first, a jazz standards album entitled *The Rest of Your Life*. The second, an all-original jazz styled album entitled *A Million Kisses* with songs about the journey and celebration of committed love—also reflected in her book *Dancing in the Kitchen*.

She has been married to her high school sweetheart, Derek, for more than thirty years and delights to be the mother of two, now grown children. Debbie spends her time performing with her jazz quartet, speaking at women's and marriage events, giving keynote concerts, and offering performance coaching in her spare time. She loves the ritual of afternoon tea and frequently pauses for a sunset to enjoy God's amazing artistry.

She and her husband are enjoying their newly emptied nest, still dancing in their kitchen and starting to cross off their bucket list. They reside in Franklin, Tennessee.

Connect with Debbie

To connect with Debbie via social media, find information on her albums, free music, receive additional *Dancing in the Kitchen* resources, or book Debbie for your next event as a speaker / featured entertainer, please go to *www.debbiecunningham.net.*

Notes

Introduction

1. *A Million Kisses*. Music and lyrics by Debbie Cunningham, © 2017 Debbie Cunningham (BMI). All rights reserved. All song lyrics throughout this book are from the album *A Million Kisses*, written and produced by Debbie Cunningham unless noted otherwise. For more information on Debbie's music, visit www.debbiecunningham.net.

Chapter 1: Dancing in the Kitchen

2. "Vivian Greene Quotes (Author)." Goodreads. https://www.goodreads.com/author/quotes/769264.Vivian_Greene.

Chapter 2: Art, Football, and Dancing

3. Cissie Graham Lynch, "Eating Ice Cream with My Grandmother," October 7, 2011, http://cissiegrahamlynch.com/eating-ice-cream-with-my-grandmother/.

4. Brené Brown. *Rising Strong: How the Ability to Reset Transforms the Way We Live, Love, Parent, and Lead.* (Random House Trade Paperbacks: Reprint edition, April 4, 2017).

Chapter 4: Learning to Hear through Grief

5. C. S. Lewis. *A Grief Observed.* (HarperOne: 1st Ed., February 6, 2001).

6. Stephen Covey. *The 7 Habits of Highly Effective People.* (DC Books: 5287th Ed., 1994).

Chapter 6: No Plan B

7. Timothy Keller. *The Meaning of Marriage: Facing the Complexities of Commitment with the Wisdom of God.* (Penguin Books: Reprint edition, November 5, 2013).

8. David B. Hampton. *After the Miracle: Illusions Along the Path to Restoration.* (Morgan James Faith: March 13, 2018).

Chapter 7: Forgiveness Changes Everything

9. Gary Chapman. *The 5 Love Languages: The Secret to Love that Lasts.* (Northfield Publishing: Reprint edition, January 1, 2015).

Chapter 8: A Marriage Arrangement

10. Swati Kumar. *The Great Indian Dilemma.* (White Falcon Publishing: August 1, 2017), https://www.goodreads.com/work/quotes/57420172-the-great-indian-dilemma.

Chapter 9: The Roommate Dilemma

11. Laura Beckder, "Marriage Quotes," *Inspirational Words of Wisdom,* https://www.wow4u.com/marriage/.

Chapter 11: Marriage and the Empty Nest

12. Barbara Rainey and Susan Yates. *Barbara and Susan's Guide to the Empty Nest.* (Bethany House Publishers: Revised, Updated edition, April 4, 2017).

13. Sheila Gregoire, "20 Two Player Games to Play with Your Husband," *To Love, Honor and Vacuum* (blog), January 17, 2013, https://tolovehonorandvacuum.com/2013/01/two-player-games-to-play-with-your-husband/.

Chapter 12: Stopping the Drift

14. Shana Schutte, "What Is the Definition of Intimacy? What Does It Mean to Be Intimate?" *Focus on the Family,* 2009, https://www.focusonthefamily.com/marriage/preparing-for-marriage/what-it-means-to-be-intimate/what-it-means-to-be-intimate.

15. Sheri Meyers, "Infidelity and Emotional Sex: How to Tell If You're Chatting or Cheating," *HuffPost,* June 25, 2012, https://www.huffingtonpost.com/sheri-meyers/infidelity-emotional-sex-technology-cheating_b_1434356.html.

Chapter 14: Celebration and Gratitude

16. Matthew Joseph Thaddeus Stepanek (July 17, 1990–June 22, 2004), known as Mattie J.T. Stepanek, American Poet, https://www.brainyquote.com/quotes/mattie_stepanek_543005.

17. "Chocolate." Music and lyrics by Debbie Cunningham. ã 2017 Debbie Cunningham (BMI). For a FREE download of the song, visit www.debbiecunningham.net.

Chapter 15: Chocolate and Dance Lessons

18. *Forrest Gump,* Directed by Robert Zemeckis (Los Angeles, CA: Paramount, 1994),https://www.imdb.com/title/tt0109830/quotes.

19. Flat Parker Project, Facebook.com, https://www.facebook.com/FlatParker/.

Morgan James
Speakers Group

We connect Morgan James published authors with live and online events and audiences who will benefit from their expertise.

Morgan James makes all of our titles available
through the Library for All Charity Organization.

www.LibraryForAll.org

CPSIA information can be obtained
at www.ICGtesting.com
Printed in the USA
JSHW081004080323
38648JS00001B/25